# Math Workbook Grades 4-5

MW00996994

## Math Book for 9-11 Year Olds

ISBN: 9798385978717

# Table of Contents

# Table of Contents

# Guidance

1) Read each question carefully before you begin answering it.

2) Attempt every question.

3) Don't spend too long on one question.

4) Check your answers.

5) Always show your workings

---

This Book Belongs to:

..................................................................................

# Place Value in very Large Numbers

A) Write each number in words.                    4 marks

1)    2,284,186 _____

_____

2)    2,222,485 _____

_____

3)    1,052,720 _____

_____

4)    1,692,733 _____

_____

B) Provide the standard notation for each value.      **3 marks**

1)    _____ seven million four hundred forty-five thousand eight hundred twenty-one

2)    _____ two million three hundred seven thousand six hundred twenty-seven

3)    _____ eight million one hundred sixty-eight thousand nine hundred sixty-three

Score: [    ]

# Place Value in very Large Numbers

A) Write each number in words.                    4 marks

1)   7,134,176   _____

_____

2)   6,154,620   _____

_____

3)   5,391,105   _____

_____

4)   7,252,006   _____

_____


B) Provide the standard notation for each value.    3 marks

1)   _____   two million three hundred ninety-two thousand seven hundred sixteen

2)   _____   four million three hundred forty-three thousand nine hundred sixty-one

3)   _____   nine million two hundred forty-four thousand nine hundred nine

Score: [    ]

Can you merge these numbers together to make one number?

1) _____    8,000,000 + 600,000 + 50,000 + 3,000 + 800 + 2

2) _____    6,000,000 + 100,000 + 40,000 + 4,000 + 500 + 40 + 5

3) _____    4,000,000 + 800,000 + 10,000 + 4,000 + 500 + 1

4) _____    2,000,000 + 300,000 + 30,000 + 9,000 + 30 + 8

5) _____    3,000,000 + 300,000 + 30,000 + 2,000 + 400 + 20 + 2

6) _____    9,000,000 + 20,000 + 2,000 + 200 + 20 + 1

7) _____    1,000,000 + 200,000 + 20,000 + 2,000 + 700 + 10 + 9

8) _____    3,000,000 + 200,000 + 3,000 + 200 + 30 + 2

Score: ☐

# Place Value in very Large Numbers

Provide the expanded notation for each value.          <u>8 marks</u>

1)   3,994,313 _____

_____

2)   2,792,713 _____

_____

3)   1,851,140 _____

_____

4)   8,935,616 _____

_____

5)   8,752,484 _____

_____

6)   1,273,444 _____

_____

7)   6,176,485 _____

_____

8)   9,420,047 _____

_____

Score: ____

Order these numbers from largest to smallest.

1)  88,988 _____
    89,463 _____
    20,476 _____
    52,427 _____

2)  53,948 _____
    49,184 _____
    99,610 _____
    76,689 _____

3)  26,491 _____
    73,152 _____
    40,066 _____
    60,016 _____

4)  41,734 _____
    80,484 _____
    21,867 _____
    54,449 _____

5)  60,457 _____
    77,355 _____
    57,456 _____
    81,407 _____

6)  25,087 _____
    63,162 _____
    54,125 _____
    78,829 _____

7)  78,602 _____
    50,275 _____
    54,075 _____
    78,817 _____

8)  67,757 _____
    86,617 _____
    73,236 _____
    43,362 _____

Score: [＿＿＿]

# Place Value in very Large Numbers

A) Compare the numbers below using < or > :     <u>16 marks</u>

1)  4,065,792___ 4,377,402   2)  8,861,196___ 9,120,903

3)  1,540,393___ 4,979,409   4)  9,527,994___ 4,043,129

5)  2,690,616___ 4,527,743   6)  9,254,582___ 3,928,595

7)  3,830,047___ 2,642,437   8)  9,658,802___ 1,769,545

9)  2,757,562___ 7,233,752   10) 2,159,855___ 9,988,235

11) 8,120,643___ 3,436,842   12) 4,079,884___ 7,851,491

13) 8,257,024___ 4,342,751   14) 2,463,038___ 2,235,806

15) 3,205,035___ 9,398,550   16) 8,973,600___ 7,872,437

Score:

Determine the place value of the underlined digit.    **10 marks**

1)  7,4<u>8</u>2,401 = _____

2)  8,3<u>4</u>6,776 = _____

3)  3,507,<u>5</u>05 = _____

4)  9,<u>6</u>99,530 = _____

5)  1,716,4<u>7</u>6 = _____

6)  2,172,2<u>2</u>3 = _____

7)  7,9<u>6</u>9,333 = _____

8)  3,860,8<u>6</u>0 = _____

9)  <u>4</u>,163,379 = _____

10) 6,531,40<u>9</u> = _____

Score: [        ]

11

Provide the place value notation for each value.      6 marks

1)  3,899,171  _____

    _____

    _____

2)  5,660,700  _____

    _____

    _____

3)  8,366,897  _____

    _____

    _____

4)  5,868,240  _____

    _____

    _____

5)  2,998,666  _____

    _____

    _____

6)  8,183,378  _____

    _____

    _____

Score: ☐

# Rounding Whole Numbers

Round these numbers to the underlined digit.      <u>20 marks</u>

1)  854,2<u>0</u>8 = _____

2)  73,<u>8</u>99 = _____

3)  <u>9</u>4,486 = _____

4)  5<u>8</u>,498 = _____

5)  813,1<u>4</u>9 = _____

6)  7,40<u>7</u>,933 = _____

7)  681,<u>2</u>29 = _____

8)  23<u>7</u>,598 = _____

9)  83<u>9</u>,255 = _____

10) 2<u>7</u>,147 = _____

11) <u>3</u>0,160 = _____

12) 5,315,3<u>6</u>2 = _____

13) 7,9<u>5</u>5,264 = _____

14) <u>4</u>10,018 = _____

15) 3<u>5</u>0,573 = _____

16) 93,1<u>2</u>6 = _____

17) 1,9<u>3</u>0,555 = _____

18) 6<u>2</u>1,619 = _____

19) 12,7<u>8</u>4 = _____

20) 63<u>0</u>,105 = _____

Score: ☐

Round these numbers to the underlined digit.

1)  <u>2</u>5,331 = _____

2)  2,16<u>4</u>,929 = _____

3)  <u>9</u>79,218 = _____

4)  1,855,7<u>3</u>4 = _____

5)  763,<u>3</u>77 = _____

6)  9,5<u>6</u>5,579 = _____

7)  8,881,<u>0</u>61 = _____

8)  695,<u>6</u>70 = _____

9)  8,1<u>5</u>4,892 = _____

10) <u>2</u>4,041 = _____

11) 49,<u>5</u>02 = _____

12) <u>4</u>7,170 = _____

13) 719,<u>8</u>09 = _____

14) 38,0<u>5</u>0 = _____

15) 2,974,<u>6</u>74 = _____

16) 53,<u>2</u>40 = _____

17) 9,66<u>9</u>,520 = _____

18) 361,6<u>2</u>3 = _____

19) <u>2</u>40,357 = _____

20) <u>3</u>61,056 = _____

Score: [￼]

Work out the answers to the calculations below. <u>**20 marks**</u>

1)  $13 - (-13) =$ _____

2)  $15 + -14 =$ _____

3)  $3 + -9 =$ _____

4)  $6 - (-13) =$ _____

5)  $-2 + 5 =$ _____

6)  $13 + -9 =$ _____

7)  $2 - (-5) =$ _____

8)  $1 - (-12) =$ _____

9)  $1 - (-9) =$ _____

10)  $1 + -7 =$ _____

11)  $12 - (-9) =$ _____

12)  $9 + -7 =$ _____

13)  $12 + -2 =$ _____

14)  $-11 + 7 =$ _____

15)  $3 + -14 =$ _____

16)  $-7 + 4 =$ _____

17)  $-9 + 3 =$ _____

18)  $5 - (-3) =$ _____

19)  $11 - (-12) =$ _____

20)  $-10 + 9 =$ _____

Score: [        ]

# Calculating with Negative Numbers

Work out the answers to the calculations below.    <u>20 marks</u>

1)    $-13 + 15 =$ _____

2)    $10 - (-3) =$ _____

3)    $13 - (-9) =$ _____

4)    $1 + -15 =$ _____

5)    $1 + -14 =$ _____

6)    $-2 + 4 =$ _____

7)    $-15 + 8 =$ _____

8)    $-6 + 13 =$ _____

9)    $-14 + 2 =$ _____

10)  $13 + -9 =$ _____

11)  $-13 + 10 =$ _____

12)  $4 - (-9) =$ _____

13)  $12 - (-11) =$ _____

14)  $9 + -3 =$ _____

15)  $12 + -1 =$ _____

16)  $-14 + 3 =$ _____

17)  $-9 + 9 =$ _____

18)  $11 + -3 =$ _____

19)  $-4 + 8 =$ _____

20)  $-10 + 15 =$ _____

Score: [＿＿]

# Calculating with Negative Numbers

Complete the operations.

1)    $4.46 -  $6.49 = _____

2)    $4.44 -  $9.66 = _____

3)    $0.61 -  $9.72 = _____

4)    $0.83 -  $9.25 = _____

5)    $7.00 -  $7.50 = _____

6)    $0.77 -  $3.27 = _____

7)    $2.77 -  $7.83 = _____

8)    $0.53 -  $2.22 = _____

9)    $0.26 -  $2.42 = _____

10)   $5.00 -  $6.00 = _____

Score: [      ]

Look at the thermometers below.

A) What are the readings on these thermometers?  1 mark

1)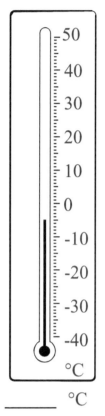

2)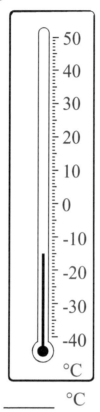

3)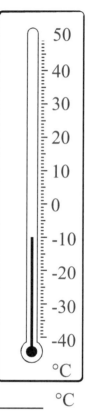

_____ °C          _____ °C          _____ °C

B) Thermometer (1) increases by 6°C. What the temperature will the termometer read now?

_____ °C   1 mark

C) Thermometer (3) decreases by 3°C. What the temperature will the termometer read now?

_____°C   1 mark

D) What is the temperature difference thermometers (2) and (3)? _____°C   1 mark

E) During a cold night, thermometer (2) drops by 8°C. What temperature will the thermometer read now?

_____°C   1 mark

Score: [ ]

# Addition and Subtraction

Add these numbers.                                      **20 marks**

1)    376        2)    84        3)    823        4)    44        5)    764
    +  30            + 70            +  21            + 86            +  61


6)    87        7)    233        8)    34        9)    328        10)   48
    + 71            +  88            + 12            +  79             + 43


11)   16        12)   12        13)   55        14)   168        15)   333
    + 38            + 50            + 34            +  73             +  92


16)   96        17)   89        18)   92        19)   530        20)   10
    + 65            + 98            + 22            +  34             + 94


Score:

Add these numbers.                                     **20 marks**

1)      1,985
   + 5,464

2)      6,381
   + 8,009

3)     70,427
   +   8,987

4)     50,283
   +   8,088

5)     41,950
   +   5,499

6)     72,020
   +   4,709

7)      7,585
   + 3,607

8)      7,829
   + 8,553

9)     63,846
   +   6,433

10)     5,171
   + 5,308

11)    13,417
   +   3,361

12)     6,203
   + 1,538

13)     4,032
   + 6,547

14)    77,771
   +   8,016

15)     9,191
   + 3,872

16)    61,410
   +   8,833

17)    43,581
   +   2,661

18)    50,433
   +   4,827

19)    59,209
   +   9,362

20)    69,779
   +   8,642

Score:

# Addition and Subtraction

Add these numbers.

1)      46,788
    +  87,821

2)      61,567
    +  27,235

3)      30,243
    +  48,152

4)      49,642
    +  77,536

5)      89,683
    +  88,298

6)      99,412
    +  53,519

7)      43,208
    +  70,123

8)      56,370
    +  73,097

9)      38,195
    +  74,489

10)     47,893
    +  95,253

11)     74,821
    +  61,847

12)     69,602
    +  61,387

13)     94,856
    +  34,179

14)     38,439
    +  74,542

15)     19,757
    +  38,544

Score:

Add these numbers.

1)  23,481
    67,250
 +  16,583

2)  79,194
    53,822
 +  22,330

3)  55,112
    86,837
 +  25,968

4)  12,050
    64,527
 +  70,367

5)  43,002
    11,892
 +  58,488

6)  67,962
    62,154
 +  88,699

7)  96,435
    85,543
 +  37,217

8)  89,780
    49,430
 +  57,339

9)  63,886
    52,054
 +  39,966

10) 76,570
    96,704
 +  90,410

11) 23,417
    34,384
 +  73,304

12) 56,240
    33,688
 +  13,305

Score:

# Addition and Subtraction

Subtract these numbers.

20 marks

1)  $\begin{array}{r} 40 \\ -\ 21 \\ \hline \end{array}$
2)  $\begin{array}{r} 98 \\ -\ 59 \\ \hline \end{array}$
3)  $\begin{array}{r} 89 \\ -\ 50 \\ \hline \end{array}$
4)  $\begin{array}{r} 82 \\ -\ 69 \\ \hline \end{array}$
5)  $\begin{array}{r} 63 \\ -\ 10 \\ \hline \end{array}$

6)  $\begin{array}{r} 53 \\ -\ 43 \\ \hline \end{array}$
7)  $\begin{array}{r} 87 \\ -\ 50 \\ \hline \end{array}$
8)  $\begin{array}{r} 26 \\ -\ 21 \\ \hline \end{array}$
9)  $\begin{array}{r} 50 \\ -\ 38 \\ \hline \end{array}$
10) $\begin{array}{r} 59 \\ -\ 58 \\ \hline \end{array}$

11) $\begin{array}{r} 61 \\ -\ 22 \\ \hline \end{array}$
12) $\begin{array}{r} 98 \\ -\ 33 \\ \hline \end{array}$
13) $\begin{array}{r} 61 \\ -\ 46 \\ \hline \end{array}$
14) $\begin{array}{r} 67 \\ -\ 14 \\ \hline \end{array}$
15) $\begin{array}{r} 91 \\ -\ 12 \\ \hline \end{array}$

16) $\begin{array}{r} 60 \\ -\ 50 \\ \hline \end{array}$
17) $\begin{array}{r} 24 \\ -\ 23 \\ \hline \end{array}$
18) $\begin{array}{r} 84 \\ -\ 40 \\ \hline \end{array}$
19) $\begin{array}{r} 63 \\ -\ 57 \\ \hline \end{array}$
20) $\begin{array}{r} 73 \\ -\ 36 \\ \hline \end{array}$

Score:

# Addition and Subtraction

Subtract these numbers. **20 marks**

1)     1,522
  -  929

2)    815
  - 604

3)    6,405
  -  239

4)    4,042
  -  147

5)    915
 - 460

6)    382
 -  44

7)    5,866
 -  647

8)    9,777
 -   47

9)    3,308
 -   19

10)   2,942
 -   76

11)   8,139
 -   93

12)   3,615
 -  877

13)   563
 -  13

14)   5,923
 -   53

15)   3,449
 -   70

16)   950
 - 689

17)   279
 -  60

18)   636
 -  13

19)   3,138
 -   52

20)   583
 - 380

Score:

# Addition and Subtraction

Subtract these numbers.                                          **15 marks**

1)     45,188
   -    4,619

2)     22,838
   -       171

3)     56,888
   -     2,130

4)      7,025
   -     4,227

5)     75,387
   -     4,532

6)     65,824
   -       196

7)      9,420
   -       823

8)     32,069
   -       280

9)     36,135
   -     5,965

10)    39,434
   -       230

11)     8,841
   -       723

12)    44,921
   -     2,273

13)    64,780
   -       850

14)    31,490
   -     2,876

15)    14,297
   -     4,400

Score:

# Addition and Subtraction

Subtract these numbers.                                    <u>15 marks</u>

1)      95,589
    -   48,829
    _____

2)      76,635
    -    3,510
    _____

3)      39,431
    -    8,791
    _____

4)      17,723
    -    4,011
    _____

5)      80,249
    -    9,736
    _____

6)      89,983
    -    1,951
    _____

7)      13,219
    -    5,580
    _____

8)      38,252
    -    5,658
    _____

9)      78,682
    -    7,657
    _____

10)     56,172
    -    1,479
    _____

11)     49,059
    -   32,480
    _____

12)     98,099
    -    4,427
    _____

13)     13,382
    -    5,699
    _____

14)     67,370
    -   29,266
    _____

15)     78,368
    -    4,597
    _____

Score:

# Multiplying and Dividing by 10, 100 and 1000

How long will it take you to complete these questions?

1)  80 × 100 = _____

2)  520 ÷ 10 = _____

3)  67 ÷ 1,000 = _____

4)  72 × 10 = _____

5)  427 ÷ 1,000 = _____

6)  93 ÷ 100 = _____

7)  559 ÷ 1,000 = _____

8)  36 × 10 = _____

9)  732 × 100 = _____

10) 64 × 100 = _____

11) 52 ÷ 10 = _____

12) 813 ÷ 1,000 = _____

13) 32 × 1,000 = _____

14) 585 × 100 = _____

15) 66 ÷ 100 = _____

16) 81 ÷ 1,000 = _____

17) 119 × 100 = _____

18) 389 ÷ 10 = _____

19) 168 × 1,000 = _____

20) 409 × 10 = _____

Score: [      ]

# Multiplying and Dividing by 10, 100 and 1000

How long will it take you to complete these questions?

1) $1,356 \times 10 =$ _____

2) $7,619 \times 1,000 =$ _____

3) $5,852 \div 100 =$ _____

4) $940 \div 10 =$ _____

5) $8,624 \div 100 =$ _____

6) $601 \times 100 =$ _____

7) $647 \div 1,000 =$ _____

8) $248 \div 1,000 =$ _____

9) $9,253 \times 10 =$ _____

10) $1,242 \times 10 =$ _____

11) $884 \div 100 =$ _____

12) $9,899 \div 10 =$ _____

13) $5,272 \div 10 =$ _____

14) $4,349 \times 100 =$ _____

15) $743 \times 1,000 =$ _____

16) $8,323 \times 1,000 =$ _____

17) $843 \div 100 =$ _____

18) $7,192 \div 100 =$ _____

19) $750 \times 1,000 =$ _____

20) $5,311 \times 1,000 =$ _____

Score:

Solve these problems using the formal written method.

1)     4,209
     ×     3
   ‾‾‾‾‾‾‾‾‾‾

2)     6,246
     ×     3
   ‾‾‾‾‾‾‾‾‾‾

3)     2,391
     ×     7
   ‾‾‾‾‾‾‾‾‾‾

4)     7,617
     ×     4
   ‾‾‾‾‾‾‾‾‾‾

5)     2,753
     ×     2
   ‾‾‾‾‾‾‾‾‾‾

6)     2,832
     ×     7
   ‾‾‾‾‾‾‾‾‾‾

7)     5,931
     ×     5
   ‾‾‾‾‾‾‾‾‾‾

8)     2,611
     ×     3
   ‾‾‾‾‾‾‾‾‾‾

9)     1,432
     ×     8
   ‾‾‾‾‾‾‾‾‾‾

10)    8,189
     ×     3
   ‾‾‾‾‾‾‾‾‾‾

11)    5,296
     ×     3
   ‾‾‾‾‾‾‾‾‾‾

12)    3,847
     ×     4
   ‾‾‾‾‾‾‾‾‾‾

Score:

Solve these problems using the formal written method.

12 marks

1)      9,941
   ×       8
   _____

2)      4,511
   ×        3
   _____

3)      8,269
   ×        5
   _____

4)      8,144
   ×        9
   _____

5)      7,189
   ×        5
   _____

6)      8,549
   ×        6
   _____

7)      7,192
   ×        4
   _____

8)      2,628
   ×        4
   _____

9)      3,911
   ×        6
   _____

10)     7,154
   ×        7
   _____

11)     8,052
   ×        4
   _____

12)     7,383
   ×        9
   _____

Score: [        ]

Solve these problems using the formal written method.

**12 marks**

1)     2,312
    ×     9

2)     7,174
    ×     8

3)     7,309
    ×     5

4)     1,127
    ×     2

5)     8,136
    ×     8

6)     4,248
    ×     7

7)     5,689
    ×     9

8)     1,051
    ×     5

9)     2,369
    ×     2

10)    5,599
    ×     4

11)    7,123
    ×     7

12)    3,733
    ×     7

Score:

Solve these problems using the formal written method.

1)     723
  ×  96

2)     800
  ×  85

3)     117
  ×  31

4)     552
  ×  55

5)     554
  ×  60

6)     321
  ×  58

7)     359
  ×  47

8)     859
  ×  24

9)     591
  ×  95

10)     807
  ×  65

11)     953
  ×  85

12)     480
  ×  60

Score:

Solve these problems using the formal written method.

12 marks

1)  218
  × 37
  ‾‾‾‾‾

2)  302
  × 51
  ‾‾‾‾‾

3)  137
  × 90
  ‾‾‾‾‾

4)  970
  × 13
  ‾‾‾‾‾

5)  739
  × 27
  ‾‾‾‾‾

6)  803
  × 53
  ‾‾‾‾‾

7)  404
  × 60
  ‾‾‾‾‾

8)  382
  × 86
  ‾‾‾‾‾

9)  552
  × 93
  ‾‾‾‾‾

10)  204
  × 16
  ‾‾‾‾‾

11)  923
  × 96
  ‾‾‾‾‾

12)  715
  × 97
  ‾‾‾‾‾

Score:

Solve these problems using the formal written method.

12 marks

1)    511
   ×  69
   ————

2)    679
   ×  60
   ————

3)    587
   ×  91
   ————

4)    340
   ×  32
   ————

5)    310
   ×  77
   ————

6)    114
   ×  21
   ————

7)    746
   ×  92
   ————

8)    894
   ×  14
   ————

9)    816
   ×  65
   ————

10)    297
    ×  44
    ————

11)    436
    ×  20
    ————

12)    475
    ×  33
    ————

Score:

# Long Multiplication

Solve these problems using the formal written method.

1)      4,677
   ×     92
      ‾‾‾‾

2)      7,000
   ×     20
      ‾‾‾‾

3)      8,024
   ×     28
      ‾‾‾‾

4)      6,478
   ×     81
      ‾‾‾‾

5)      8,727
   ×     37
      ‾‾‾‾

6)      7,161
   ×     19
      ‾‾‾‾

7)      9,776
   ×     23
      ‾‾‾‾

8)      7,412
   ×     41
      ‾‾‾‾

9)      9,120
   ×     89
      ‾‾‾‾

10)      7,698
   ×     16
      ‾‾‾‾

11)      9,362
   ×     69
      ‾‾‾‾

12)      6,932
   ×     20
      ‾‾‾‾

Score: [      ]

Solve these problems using the formal written method.

12 marks

1)  4,509
  × 98
  _____

2)  8,502
  × 45
  _____

3)  9,128
  × 71
  _____

4)  1,481
  × 45
  _____

5)  2,987
  × 39
  _____

6)  1,094
  × 28
  _____

7)  9,106
  × 63
  _____

8)  2,734
  × 38
  _____

9)  1,357
  × 79
  _____

10)  2,780
  × 61
  _____

11)  8,620
  × 86
  _____

12)  1,495
  × 32
  _____

Score: ____

Solve these problems using the formal written method.

**12 marks**

1)    4,370
    ×    80
   ‾‾‾‾‾‾‾‾

2)    3,626
    ×    66
   ‾‾‾‾‾‾‾‾

3)    2,509
    ×    78
   ‾‾‾‾‾‾‾‾

4)    7,450
    ×    49
   ‾‾‾‾‾‾‾‾

5)    9,318
    ×    41
   ‾‾‾‾‾‾‾‾

6)    3,847
    ×    59
   ‾‾‾‾‾‾‾‾

7)    9,305
    ×    13
   ‾‾‾‾‾‾‾‾

8)    9,009
    ×    80
   ‾‾‾‾‾‾‾‾

9)    3,846
    ×    89
   ‾‾‾‾‾‾‾‾

10)    5,938
     ×    36
    ‾‾‾‾‾‾‾‾

11)    7,187
     ×    70
    ‾‾‾‾‾‾‾‾

12)    4,723
     ×    97
    ‾‾‾‾‾‾‾‾

Score:

Solve these problems using the formal written method.

1)  4,421
    ×    85

2)  3,271
    ×    50

3)  7,424
    ×    76

4)  6,131
    ×    60

5)  1,454
    ×    40

6)  4,880
    ×    28

7)  9,700
    ×    86

8)  9,370
    ×    19

9)  2,432
    ×    35

10) 9,404
    ×    42

11) 7,748
    ×    34

12) 8,996
    ×    81

Score:

Solve these problems using the formal written method.

**12 marks**

1)

5) 9,800

2)

4) 4,568

3)

8) 5,928

4)

8) 7,320

5)

4) 3,152

6)

4) 8,632

7)

3) 1,272

8)

7) 2,870

9)

8) 9,208

10)

3) 4,800

11)

7) 9,198

12)

4) 5,476

Score:

Solve these problems using the formal written method.

1)
$$4 \overline{)3,944}$$

2)
$$5 \overline{)5,305}$$

3)
$$3 \overline{)6,948}$$

4)
$$8 \overline{)7,432}$$

5)
$$8 \overline{)1,216}$$

6)
$$7 \overline{)7,707}$$

7)
$$2 \overline{)6,554}$$

8)
$$7 \overline{)6,930}$$

9)
$$5 \overline{)1,570}$$

10)
$$8 \overline{)3,600}$$

11)
$$3 \overline{)1,845}$$

12)
$$3 \overline{)1,521}$$

Score:

Solve these problems using the formal written method.

1)

$3 \overline{)\ 2,766}$

2)

$2 \overline{)\ 2,730}$

3)

$9 \overline{)\ 9,936}$

4)

$7 \overline{)\ 9,667}$

5)

$7 \overline{)\ 4,928}$

6)

$2 \overline{)\ 1,506}$

7)

$2 \overline{)\ 9,806}$

8)

$8 \overline{)\ 7,456}$

9)

$3 \overline{)\ 2,313}$

10)

$8 \overline{)\ 4,864}$

11)

$9 \overline{)\ 5,625}$

12)

$8 \overline{)\ 9,936}$

Score:

# Long Division with no Remainders

Solve these problems using the formal written method. **12 marks**

1) $75\overline{)975}$

2) $97\overline{)679}$

3) $21\overline{)441}$

4) $47\overline{)329}$

5) $39\overline{)195}$

6) $93\overline{)372}$

7) $27\overline{)756}$

8) $93\overline{)558}$

9) $70\overline{)140}$

10) $86\overline{)688}$

11) $97\overline{)873}$

12) $40\overline{)640}$

Score: ______

Solve these problems using the formal written method.

12 marks

1)

$66 \overline{)792}$

2)

$15 \overline{)480}$

3)   $50 \overline{)100}$

4)

$35 \overline{)840}$

5)

$68 \overline{)884}$

6)

$13 \overline{)390}$

7)

$56 \overline{)280}$

8)

$55 \overline{)880}$

9)

$70 \overline{)840}$

10)

$60 \overline{)600}$

11)

$87 \overline{)696}$

12)

$59 \overline{)472}$

Score:

# Long Division with no Remainders

Solve these problems using the formal written method. **12 marks**

1) $86\overline{)86}$

2) $97\overline{)485}$

3) $53\overline{)530}$

4) $13\overline{)273}$

5) $57\overline{)969}$

6) $71\overline{)355}$

7) $89\overline{)890}$

8) $82\overline{)328}$

9) $32\overline{)704}$

10) $29\overline{)203}$

11) $50\overline{)750}$

12) $43\overline{)473}$

Score:

# Long Division with no Remainders

Solve these problems using the formal written method.

**12 marks**

1)

$55 \overline{)7{,}425}$

2)

$58 \overline{)9{,}744}$

3) $62 \overline{)4{,}526}$

4)

$56 \overline{)6{,}720}$

5)

$81 \overline{)9{,}801}$

6)

$87 \overline{)1{,}218}$

7)

$20 \overline{)5{,}940}$

8)

$96 \overline{)2{,}592}$

9)

$77 \overline{)6{,}468}$

10)

$55 \overline{)9{,}790}$

11)

$99 \overline{)8{,}316}$

12)

$44 \overline{)6{,}644}$

Score:

Solve these problems using the formal written method.

1)

$98 \overline{)\, 2{,}450}$

2)

$23 \overline{)\, 5{,}060}$

3)

$76 \overline{)\, 6{,}156}$

4)

$27 \overline{)\, 4{,}536}$

5)

$27 \overline{)\, 3{,}213}$

6)

$33 \overline{)\, 9{,}801}$

7)

$25 \overline{)\, 7{,}075}$

8)

$63 \overline{)\, 1{,}953}$

9)

$68 \overline{)\, 8{,}636}$

10)

$20 \overline{)\, 9{,}260}$

11)

$40 \overline{)\, 5{,}400}$

12)

$94 \overline{)\, 6{,}016}$

Score:

Solve these problems using the formal written method.    __12 marks__

1)

$81\overline{)646}$

2)

$17\overline{)720}$

3)

$31\overline{)654}$

4)

$20\overline{)348}$

5)

$37\overline{)575}$

6)

$87\overline{)362}$

7)

$65\overline{)658}$

8)

$17\overline{)908}$

9)

$21\overline{)820}$

10)

$67\overline{)960}$

11)

$36\overline{)856}$

12)

$82\overline{)175}$

Score:

# Long Division with Remainders

Solve these problems using the formal written method. **12 marks**

1) $35\overline{)463}$

2) $78\overline{)208}$

3) $30\overline{)441}$

4) $69\overline{)421}$

5) $74\overline{)687}$

6) $89\overline{)853}$

7) $34\overline{)872}$

8) $86\overline{)939}$

9) $48\overline{)381}$

10) $43\overline{)990}$

11) $91\overline{)671}$

12) $25\overline{)312}$

Score:

# Long Division with Remainders

Solve these problems using the formal written method.

**12 marks**

1)

$59 \overline{)662}$

2)

$18 \overline{)615}$

3)

$86 \overline{)164}$

4)

$49 \overline{)659}$

5)

$33 \overline{)108}$

6)

$42 \overline{)832}$

7)

$31 \overline{)439}$

8)

$84 \overline{)926}$

9)

$44 \overline{)644}$

10)

$77 \overline{)203}$

11)

$88 \overline{)637}$

12)

$36 \overline{)571}$

Score:

# Long Division with Remainders

Solve these problems using the formal written method. **12 marks**

1) $18\overline{)377}$

2) $80\overline{)835}$

3) $95\overline{)638}$

4) $69\overline{)728}$

5) $76\overline{)436}$

6) $64\overline{)450}$

7) $16\overline{)226}$

8) $77\overline{)863}$

9) $79\overline{)572}$

10) $96\overline{)734}$

11) $44\overline{)897}$

12) $70\overline{)600}$

Score:

# Long Division with Remainders

Solve these problems using the formal written method.

**12 marks**

1)

$55 \overline{)7,042}$

2)

$55 \overline{)866}$

3)

$38 \overline{)2,431}$

4)

$57 \overline{)306}$

5)

$29 \overline{)3,696}$

6)

$29 \overline{)7,289}$

7)

$45 \overline{)7,178}$

8)

$73 \overline{)5,094}$

9)

$36 \overline{)9,500}$

10)

$38 \overline{)8,581}$

11)

$74 \overline{)3,687}$

12)

$58 \overline{)559}$

Score:

# Long Division with Remainders

Solve these problems using the formal written method. **12 marks**

1) $19\overline{)9{,}544}$

2) $18\overline{)8{,}484}$

3) $56\overline{)538}$

4) $25\overline{)870}$

5) $16\overline{)6{,}001}$

6) $94\overline{)845}$

7) $32\overline{)6{,}755}$

8) $43\overline{)7{,}375}$

9) $60\overline{)2{,}778}$

10) $16\overline{)3{,}441}$

11) $36\overline{)154}$

12) $97\overline{)187}$

Score:

# Long Division with Remainders

Solve these problems using the formal written method.

**12 marks**

1)

$52\overline{)8,338}$

2)

$18\overline{)1,885}$

3)

$21\overline{)2,195}$

4)

$38\overline{)4,122}$

5)

$54\overline{)7,318}$

6)

$79\overline{)9,911}$

7)

$93\overline{)9,548}$

8)

$82\overline{)5,365}$

9)

$43\overline{)1,813}$

10)

$89\overline{)6,574}$

11)

$76\overline{)7,326}$

12)

$23\overline{)5,510}$

Score:

A) Divide these numbers. Each problem have a remainder.

**6 marks**

1)  $79 \overline{)\ 9,835}$

2)  $45 \overline{)\ 3,719}$

3)  $95 \overline{)\ 1,628}$

4)  $67 \overline{)\ 7,620}$

5)  $94 \overline{)\ 4,197}$

6)  $61 \overline{)\ 6,659}$

B) Solve.

**2 marks**

1)  How many 13 cm pieces of rope can you cut from a rope that is 208 cm long?

_____

2)  Donald is reading a book with 220 pages. If Donald wants to read the same number of pages every day, how many pages would Donald have to read each day to finish in 10 days?

_____

Score: [　　　]

Use the distributive property to fill the missing values.    **10 marks**

1)    $( 5 + 29 ) \times \underline{\quad} = 16 \times 5 + 16 \times \underline{\quad}$

2)    $( 16 + 11 ) \times \underline{\quad} = 13 \times 16 + 13 \times \underline{\quad}$

3)    $( \underline{\quad} + 13 ) \times 22 = 22 \times 3 + \underline{\quad} \times 13$

4)    $( \underline{\quad} + 29 ) \times 9 = 9 \times 17 + \underline{\quad} \times 29$

5)    $18 \times ( 9 + \underline{\quad} ) = 18 \times \underline{\quad} + 18 \times 3$

6)    $3 \times ( \underline{\quad} + 8 ) = 3 \times 10 + \underline{\quad} \times 8$

7)    $16 \times ( \underline{\quad} + 24 ) = 16 \times 27 + \underline{\quad} \times 24$

8)    $( \underline{\quad} + 16 ) \times 4 = 4 \times 20 + \underline{\quad} \times 16$

9)    $7 \times ( 28 + \underline{\quad} ) = 7 \times \underline{\quad} + 7 \times 16$

10)    $( \underline{\quad} + 11 ) \times 30 = 30 \times 19 + 30 \times \underline{\quad}$

Score:

Use the distributive property to fill the missing values.

**10 marks**

1)  $\_\_ \times ( 24 + 20 ) = 15 \times 24 + 15 \times \_\_$

2)  $( 5 + \_ ) \times 18 = 18 \times \_ + 18 \times 4$

3)  $( \_\_ + 16 ) \times 28 = 28 \times 15 + \_\_ \times 16$

4)  $13 \times ( \_\_ + 23 ) = 13 \times 14 + 13 \times \_\_$

5)  $( 28 + 5 ) \times \_ = 4 \times 28 + 4 \times \_$

6)  $14 \times ( \_\_ + 4 ) = 14 \times 13 + 14 \times \_$

7)  $( 7 + \_\_ ) \times 25 = 25 \times \_ + 25 \times 21$

8)  $( 12 + \_ ) \times 3 = 3 \times \_\_ + 3 \times 8$

9)  $( 8 + \_\_ ) \times 14 = 14 \times \_ + 14 \times 15$

10) $18 \times ( 25 + \_\_ ) = 18 \times 25 + \_\_ \times 23$

Score:

# Mental Calculations

A) Work out the additions mentally. Write your answer.                    <u>**10 marks**</u>

1)   15 + 12 = [　　　　]        2)   33 + 68 = [　　　　]

3)   81 + 90 = [　　　　]        4)   43 + 56 = [　　　　]

5)   66 + 50 = [　　　　]        6)   75 + 45 = [　　　　]

7)   16 + 60 = [　　　　]        8)   36 + 90 = [　　　　]

9)   55 + 98 = [　　　　]        10)  81 + 42 = [　　　　]

B) Work out the subtractions mentally.                    <u>**10 marks**</u>

1)   20 - 13 = [　　　　]        2)   37 - 24 = [　　　　]

3)   51 - 17 = [　　　　]        4)   52 - 15 = [　　　　]

5)   53 - 42 = [　　　　]        6)   49 - 24 = [　　　　]

7)   65 - 20 = [　　　　]        8)   52 - 34 = [　　　　]

9)   56 - 27 = [　　　　]        10)  30 - 15 = [　　　　]

Score: [　　　]

# Mental Calculations

A) Solve these problems mentally.    <u>10 marks</u>

1)  $30 \times 10 =$ _____    2)  $21 \times 60 =$ _____

3)  $43 \times 40 =$ _____    4)  $44 \times 60 =$ _____

5)  $19 \times 80 =$ _____    6)  $42 \times 10 =$ _____

7)  $53 \times 90 =$ _____    8)  $88 \times 70 =$ _____

9)  $57 \times 60 =$ _____    10) $32 \times 50 =$ _____

B) Work out the following calculations mentally.    <u>10 marks</u>

1)  $11 - 8 + 4 - 2 =$ _____    2)  $10 + 20 - 3 - 10 =$ ___

3)  $15 + 9 - 6 - 2 =$ _____    4)  $15 - 5 + 7 - 2 =$ _____

5)  $14 + 2 - 4 - 9 =$ _____    6)  $18 + 17 - 7 - 10 =$ ___

7)  $18 - 8 + 15 - 2 =$ _____    8)  $10 + 2 - 8 - 1 =$ _____

9)  $20 - 9 + 15 - 2 =$ _____    10) $18 - 5 - 6 + 2 =$ _____

Score: [     ]

# Mental Calculations

Write the missing numbers.    20 marks

1)  $\boxed{\phantom{00}} + 92 = 157$

2)  $\boxed{\phantom{00}} + 41 = 117$

3)  $34 + \boxed{\phantom{00}} = 107$

4)  $97 + \boxed{\phantom{00}} = 146$

5)  $57 + 22 = \boxed{\phantom{00}}$

6)  $63 + \boxed{\phantom{00}} = 156$

7)  $\boxed{\phantom{00}} + 70 = 108$

8)  $62 + \boxed{\phantom{00}} = 85$

9)  $\boxed{\phantom{00}} + 29 = 64$

10)  $\boxed{\phantom{00}} + 70 = 81$

11)  $\boxed{\phantom{00}} - 17 = 27$

12)  $\boxed{\phantom{00}} - 17 = 15$

13)  $54 - \boxed{\phantom{00}} = 2$

14)  $88 - \boxed{\phantom{00}} = 32$

15)  $74 - \boxed{\phantom{00}} = 6$

16)  $29 - \boxed{\phantom{00}} = 4$

17)  $21 - \boxed{\phantom{00}} = 11$

18)  $\boxed{\phantom{00}} - 39 = 10$

19)  $\boxed{\phantom{00}} - 15 = 24$

20)  $63 - \boxed{\phantom{00}} = 23$

Score: $\boxed{\phantom{00}}$

Fill in the missing numbers in these calculations.   <u>20 marks</u>

1) [ ] × 59 = 295

2) 8 × [ ] = 144

3) 5 × [ ] = 185

4) 9 × [ ] = 531

5) [ ] × 46 = 230

6) [ ] × 72 = 216

7) [ ] × 24 = 144

8) [ ] × 18 = 126

9) [ ] × 31 = 279

10) 4 × [ ] = 104

11) [ ] ÷ 9 = 29

12) [ ] ÷ 9 = 17

13) 69 ÷ [ ] = 23

14) [ ] ÷ 6 = 20

15) [ ] ÷ 3 = 15

16) [ ] ÷ 8 = 20

17) [ ] ÷ 7 = 16

18) [ ] ÷ 5 = 16

19) 126 ÷ [ ] = 21

20) [ ] ÷ 8 = 29

Score: [ ]

Join each of these calculations to the correct answer.

a. 67 - 21 = _____ •

b. 39 × 16 = _____ •

c. 82 + 88 = _____ •

d. 825 ÷ 11 = _____ •

e. 99 - 59 = _____ •

f. 43 - 28 = _____ •

g. 69 + 33 = _____ •

h. 54 - 22 = _____ •

i. 95 + 36 = _____ •

j. 59 - 16 = _____ •

k. 60 + 48 = _____ •

• F = 40

• H = 102

• J = 170

• K = 131

• B = 624

• A = 108

• E = 15

• G = 46

• D = 75

• I = 43

• C = 32

Score: ___

Write in the missing signs: $+ \ - \ \times \ \div$    **16 marks**

1)  12___ 20___ 4 = 960

2)  (14___ 19)___ 5 = 6.6

3)  10___ 5___ 5 = 20

4)  3___ 12___ 4___ 18 = 37

5)  3___ 17___ 16 = 36

6)  12___ 10___ 20 = 2,400

7)  (19___ 17)___ 12 = 3

8)  (14___ 8)___ 9 = 121

9)  10___ (19___ 19) = 380

10)  9___ 19___ 16 = 44

11)  (11___ 5)___ 16 = 1

12)  14___ (13___ 11) = 336

13)  18___ 6___ 14___ 7 = 17

14)  19___ 3___ 2 = 114

15)  7___ 12___ 20___ 11 = 10

16)  8___ (19___ 2) = 168

Score: [        ]

# Multiples, Factors and Prime Numbers

A) List all the factors of the following numbers.    **6 marks**

1)   4 _____

2)   50 _____

3)   3 _____

4)   10 _____

5)   97 _____

6)   36 _____

B) Find the greatest common factor of the following    **3 marks**
sets of numbers.

1)   21 _____    __

     12 _____

2)   12 _____    __

      6 _____

3)   51 _____    __

     30 _____

C) List the prime factors for each number. Is the    **3 marks**
number prime?

1)   19 = **19 (Yes)**

2)   63 = _____

3)   9 = _____

4)   67 = _____

Score: [    ]

# Multiples, Factors and Prime Numbers

A) List the first four multiples of each number.    <u>10 marks</u>

1)    2 _____

2)    3 _____

3)    4 _____

4)    31 _____

5)    92 _____

6)    5 _____

7)    53 _____

8)    76 _____

9)    7 _____

10)    1 _____

B) Circle all the numbers that are multiples of both    <u>2 marks</u>
3 and 7.

    49        14        21        42        57

C) Tick the numbers that are common factors of    <u>2 marks</u>
12 and 18.

    6        9        36        2        4

D) Circle the prime numbers.    <u>3 marks</u>

  72      47      97      65      23      95

E) Identify the prime numbers between 50 and 100.    <u>10 marks</u>

_____

_____    Score: [    ]

Draw a line to match the following calculations to their correct answer.

1) $3 + 9 + 18 + 2$                        330

2) $(19 \times 4) - (2 + 19)$              55

3) $(12 + 2) \div 2$                       31

4) $(9 + 2) \times (20 + 10)$             341

5) $(10 \times 14) - (20 + 20)$           32

6) $10 + 6 + 3 \times 5$                   7

7) $13 \times (10 + 13)$                  100

8) $16 + 3^2$                              96

9) $11 \times (18 + 13)$                   25

10) $8 \times (2 + 10)$                   299

Score:

A) Which two calculations give the same answer?          <u>2 marks</u>

1)  $3 + 4 \times 9$

2)  $(3 + 4) \times 9$          _____ and _____

3)  $3 + (4 \times 9)$

B) Amira has 5 boxes.          <u>1 mark</u>

There are 12 balls in each box.

She takes three balls out of each box.

Circle the calculation that shows the total number of balls

in the boxes now.

1)  $(5 \times 12) - 3$          2)  $5 \times (12 - 3)$          3)  $5 \times 12 - 3$

C) Work out the missing numbers.          <u>4 marks</u>

1)  $3 + 6 \times \boxed{\phantom{0}} - 9 = 6$          2)  $4^2 + \boxed{\phantom{0}} - 2 \times 3 = 18$

3)  $\boxed{\phantom{0}} + (9 - 6) \times 5 = 22$          4)  $3 + (4 \times 9) - \boxed{\phantom{0}} = 27$

Score: $\boxed{\phantom{00}}$

# Order of Operations (BODMAS)

Use your knowledge of BODMAS to solve these problems.

1) $2 \times (9 + 2) =$ _____

2) $0 \times 12 + 10 =$ _____

3) $6 \times (2 + 12) =$ _____

4) $11 \times 10 - 10 =$ _____

5) $(3 \times 11) - (12 + 4) =$ _____

6) $7 + 12 - 6 + 5 =$ _____

7) $0 \times 10 + 5 =$ _____

8) $8 + 11 \times 4 =$ _____

9) $11 + 5 \times 2 =$ _____

10) $10 \times (6 + 0) =$ _____

Score: ☐

Use your knowledge of BODMAS to solve these problems.

1)    $(5 + 8) \div 9 =$ _____    2)    $4 + 11 \times 0 + 9 =$ _____

3)    $(0 + 8) \div 8 =$ _____    4)    $6 \times (8 + 5) =$ _____

5)    $(5 + 3) \div 2 =$ _____    6)    $4 + 8 + 5 \times 7 =$ _____

7)    $4 + 10 + 0 + 9 =$ _____    8)    $(11 + 3) \times (8 + 6) =$ _____

9)    $10 + 1 + 4 \times 3 =$ _____    10)    $(6 + 1) \times (2 + 12) =$ _____

Score: [      ]

Use your knowledge of BODMAS to solve these problems.          <u>**10 marks**</u>

1)    $18 \times (3 + 2) =$ _____   2)   $(14 \times 12) - (3 + 8) =$ _____

3)    $2 \times 3 \times 17 =$ _____   4)   $4 + 17 + 2 + 14 =$ _____

5)    $(15 + 11) \times 4 =$ _____   6)   $12 \times (5 + 19) =$ _____

7)    $(20 + 14) \times (1 + 2) =$ _____   8)   $19 + 17 + 17 =$ _____

9)    $13 + 12 + 14 + 3 =$ _____   10)  $16 \times 9 - 9 =$ _____

Score: [          ]

Find the answer to these calculations.                    **10 marks**

1)   $(16 + 10) \times (10 + 3) =$ _____

2)   $(5 + 4) \div 3 =$ _____

3)   $(5 \times 18) - (10 + 18) =$ _____

4)   $(15 + 5) \times (3 + 1) =$ _____

5)   $15 - 4^2 =$ _____

6)   $6 + 5 \times 6 - 5 =$ _____

7)   $10 + 10 \times 10 - 10 =$ _____

8)   $(15 + 9) \times (8 + 10) =$ _____

9)   $17 + 11 + 2 =$ _____

10)  $(1 \times 8) - (1 + 14) =$ _____

Score:

# Calculations Problems

Solve the following calculations.                          <u>12 marks</u>

1)       215
     ×   68


2)      9,377
     +  4,762


3)        813
     ×    78


4)      85,757
     -   4,944


5)      75,166
     -   1,722


6)      32,981
     -   3,967


7)
     54)‾1,620


8)
     17)‾357


9)      14,006
     +   5,484


10)
     25)‾22


11)       220
      ×    17


12)      7,021
      +  5,852


Score: ☐

A) Complete each family of facts.                          <u>8 marks</u>

1)                                                      2)

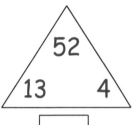                                    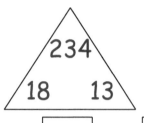

| □ | × | □ | = | □ |    | □ | × | □ | = | □ |
| □ | × | □ | = | □ |    | □ | × | □ | = | □ |
| □ | ÷ | □ | = | □ |    | □ | ÷ | □ | = | □ |
| □ | ÷ | □ | = | □ |    | □ | ÷ | □ | = | □ |

B) Work out the following calculations mentally.     <u>3 marks</u>

1)   52 - 11 - 21 + 24 =

2)   38 + 57 - 13 - 2 =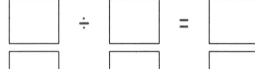

3)   44 - 18 + 14 - 3 = ———————————

C) Join each of these calculations to the correct     <u>4 marks</u>
answer.

   a.  3,843 ÷ 61   •                      • A= 63

   b.  29 - 29      •                      • B= 59

   c.  15 + 44      •                      • C= 80

   d.  7,600 ÷ 95   •                      • D= 0

Score: □

Write the following fractions in their simplest form. **15 marks**

1) $\dfrac{33}{36}$ =

2) $\dfrac{128}{160}$ =

3) $\dfrac{54}{72}$ =

4) $\dfrac{54}{96}$ =

5) $\dfrac{8}{40}$ =

6) $\dfrac{4}{14}$ =

7) $\dfrac{9}{54}$ =

8) $\dfrac{21}{27}$ =

9) $\dfrac{10}{12}$ =

10) $\dfrac{88}{96}$ =

11) $\dfrac{15}{20}$ =

12) $\dfrac{126}{144}$ =

13) $\dfrac{2}{6}$ =

14) $\dfrac{30}{55}$ =

15) $\dfrac{32}{40}$ =

Score:

# Simplifying Fractions

Write the following fractions in their simplest form.  <u>15 marks</u>

1)  $\dfrac{2}{4}$ =

2)  $\dfrac{24}{40}$ =

3)  $\dfrac{14}{84}$ =

4)  $\dfrac{102}{192}$ =

5)  $\dfrac{32}{56}$ =

6)  $\dfrac{3}{6}$ =

7)  $\dfrac{24}{36}$ =

8)  $\dfrac{14}{77}$ =

9)  $\dfrac{4}{12}$ =

10)  $\dfrac{39}{54}$ =

11)  $\dfrac{36}{90}$ =

12)  $\dfrac{24}{27}$ =

13)  $\dfrac{15}{24}$ =

14)  $\dfrac{36}{96}$ =

15)  $\dfrac{102}{120}$ =

Score:

Write the following fractions in their simplest form. **15 marks**

1) $\dfrac{144}{288}$ =

2) $\dfrac{42}{140}$ =

3) $\dfrac{5}{10}$ =

4) $\dfrac{14}{126}$ =

5) $\dfrac{4}{12}$ =

6) $\dfrac{21}{56}$ =

7) $\dfrac{20}{25}$ =

8) $\dfrac{36}{108}$ =

9) $\dfrac{15}{30}$ =

10) $\dfrac{15}{18}$ =

11) $\dfrac{42}{54}$ =

12) $\dfrac{9}{21}$ =

13) $\dfrac{52}{96}$ =

14) $\dfrac{18}{66}$ =

15) $\dfrac{40}{256}$ =

Score: [ ]

# Simplifying Fractions

Write the following fractions in their simplest form. <u>15 marks</u>

1) $\dfrac{189}{900}$ =

2) $\dfrac{12}{18}$ =

3) $\dfrac{8}{12}$ =

4) $\dfrac{36}{63}$ =

5) $\dfrac{18}{30}$ =

6) $\dfrac{9}{81}$ =

7) $\dfrac{104}{160}$ =

8) $\dfrac{4}{32}$ =

9) $\dfrac{6}{36}$ =

10) $\dfrac{8}{16}$ =

11) $\dfrac{21}{35}$ =

12) $\dfrac{84}{108}$ =

13) $\dfrac{20}{50}$ =

14) $\dfrac{27}{180}$ =

15) $\dfrac{9}{36}$ =

Score:

Compare each pair of fractions using the >, < or = symbols.    <u>12 marks</u>

1)  $\dfrac{25}{18}$    $\dfrac{2}{4}$

2)  $\dfrac{2}{9}$    $\dfrac{2}{10}$

3)  $6\dfrac{1}{3}$    $\dfrac{6}{10}$

4)  $\dfrac{21}{33}$    $\dfrac{3}{2}$

5)  $\dfrac{18}{8}$    $\dfrac{80}{32}$

6)  $\dfrac{2}{22}$    $\dfrac{7}{3}$

7)  $\dfrac{7}{8}$    $\dfrac{6}{24}$

8)  $\dfrac{8}{10}$    $\dfrac{3}{32}$

9)  $\dfrac{7}{9}$    $5\dfrac{6}{12}$

10)  $\dfrac{29}{18}$    $\dfrac{4}{7}$

11)  $\dfrac{14}{10}$    $\dfrac{17}{6}$

12)  $\dfrac{5}{10}$    $\dfrac{70}{120}$

Score:

Compare each pair of fractions using the >, < or = symbols.    <u>12 marks</u>

1)    $4\dfrac{5}{6}$    $\dfrac{12}{8}$

2)    $\dfrac{6}{12}$    $2\dfrac{5}{7}$

3)    $\dfrac{6}{9}$    $\dfrac{6}{11}$

4)    $\dfrac{3}{5}$    $\dfrac{9}{10}$

5)    $\dfrac{9}{12}$    $\dfrac{15}{30}$

6)    $4\dfrac{8}{12}$    $\dfrac{6}{5}$

7)    $1\dfrac{7}{8}$    $\dfrac{3}{2}$

8)    $\dfrac{5}{55}$    $7\dfrac{2}{3}$

9)    $6\dfrac{8}{9}$    $\dfrac{6}{7}$

10)    $\dfrac{10}{4}$    $\dfrac{2}{4}$

11)    $\dfrac{6}{12}$    $\dfrac{2}{3}$

12)    $3\dfrac{7}{11}$    $\dfrac{15}{9}$

Score:

# Ordering and Comparing Fractions

Order each set of fractions from smallest to largest.

1)   $5\dfrac{1}{3}$    $6\dfrac{1}{3}$    $7\dfrac{1}{3}$    $4\dfrac{1}{3}$    $3\dfrac{1}{3}$    <u>5 marks</u>

3 |—————————————————————————————| 8

2)   $3$   $4\dfrac{4}{5}$    $4\dfrac{1}{5}$    $3\dfrac{3}{5}$    $2\dfrac{1}{5}$    <u>5 marks</u>

2 |—————————————————————————————| 5

3)   $3$   $5\dfrac{1}{2}$    $4\dfrac{1}{2}$    $4$   $2\dfrac{1}{2}$    <u>5 marks</u>

2 |—————————————————————————————| 7

4)   $11\dfrac{1}{5}$    $10\dfrac{1}{5}$    $12\dfrac{2}{5}$    $11\dfrac{4}{5}$    $10\dfrac{7}{10}$    <u>5 marks</u>

10 |—————————————————————————————| 13

Score: [    ]

Order each set of fractions from smallest to largest.

1)   $20$   $19\frac{1}{3}$   $22\frac{1}{3}$   $21\frac{1}{3}$   $20\frac{2}{3}$

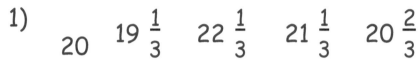

2)   $7\frac{1}{4}$   $4\frac{1}{4}$   $8\frac{1}{2}$   $5\frac{1}{2}$   $6\frac{1}{4}$

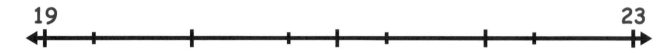

3)   $4\frac{3}{10}$   $5\frac{3}{5}$   $6\frac{2}{5}$   $4\frac{4}{5}$   $6\frac{7}{10}$

4)   $7$   $5\frac{1}{5}$   $7\frac{3}{5}$   $5\frac{4}{5}$   $6\frac{2}{5}$

Score:

# Adding and Subtracting Fractions

A) Add these fractions. Give your answers to the calculations below in the simplest form.    <u>**6 marks**</u>

1) $\dfrac{6}{10} + \dfrac{5}{10} =$

2) $\dfrac{1}{2} + \dfrac{14}{32} =$

3) $\dfrac{2}{4} + \dfrac{2}{16} =$

4) $\dfrac{9}{12} + \dfrac{1}{2} =$

5) $\dfrac{5}{7} + \dfrac{1}{3} =$

6) $\dfrac{2}{6} + \dfrac{6}{7} =$

B) Subtract these fractions. Give your answers to the calculations below in the simplest form.    <u>**6 marks**</u>

1) $\dfrac{10}{14} - \dfrac{2}{3} =$

2) $\dfrac{7}{8} - \dfrac{5}{11} =$

3) $\dfrac{9}{10} - \dfrac{1}{2} =$

4) $\dfrac{2}{8} - \dfrac{1}{5} =$

5) $\dfrac{9}{16} - \dfrac{1}{12} =$

6) $\dfrac{3}{7} - \dfrac{3}{8} =$

Score:

# Adding and Subtracting Fractions

A) Subtract these improper fractions. Leave your answer as an improper fraction.   6 marks

1)  $\dfrac{93}{10} - \dfrac{63}{10} =$

2)  $\dfrac{76}{9} - \dfrac{59}{9} =$

3)  $\dfrac{19}{2} - \dfrac{7}{2} =$

4)  $\dfrac{29}{3} - \dfrac{28}{3} =$

5)  $\dfrac{33}{4} - \dfrac{7}{4} =$

6)  $\dfrac{69}{7} - \dfrac{68}{7} =$

B) Add these fractions. Leave your answer as an improper fraction.   6 marks

1)  $\dfrac{86}{14} + \dfrac{75}{14} =$

2)  $\dfrac{67}{9} + \dfrac{51}{9} =$

3)  $\dfrac{71}{12} + \dfrac{56}{12} =$

4)  $\dfrac{43}{8} + \dfrac{14}{8} =$

5)  $\dfrac{70}{18} + \dfrac{39}{18} =$

6)  $\dfrac{64}{7} + \dfrac{37}{7} =$

Score:

A) Add these fractions. Give your answers as mixed numbers.    <u>6 marks</u>

1)  $6 \dfrac{3}{14} + \dfrac{5}{32} =$

2)  $5 \dfrac{1}{8} + \dfrac{2}{3} =$

3)  $2 \dfrac{3}{16} + \dfrac{9}{10} =$

4)  $9 \dfrac{1}{2} + \dfrac{1}{6} =$

5)  $9 \dfrac{4}{9} + \dfrac{4}{5} =$

6)  $1 \dfrac{5}{8} + \dfrac{2}{3} =$

B) Subtract these fractions. Give your answers as mixed numbers.    <u>6 marks</u>

1)  $9 \dfrac{3}{5} - \dfrac{9}{11} =$

2)  $8 \dfrac{9}{10} - \dfrac{1}{9} =$

3)  $9 \dfrac{1}{10} - \dfrac{1}{6} =$

4)  $4 \dfrac{1}{6} - \dfrac{2}{5} =$

5)  $5 \dfrac{2}{5} - \dfrac{1}{4} =$

6)  $9 \dfrac{1}{4} - \dfrac{6}{7} =$

Score:

A) Add these fractions. Give your answers as mixed <u>6 marks</u> numbers.

1) $6\dfrac{7}{18} + 1\dfrac{3}{8} =$

2) $7\dfrac{9}{10} + 9\dfrac{4}{9} =$

3) $7\dfrac{2}{3} + 7\dfrac{1}{3} =$

4) $8\dfrac{9}{14} + 7\dfrac{3}{5} =$

5) $5\dfrac{3}{7} + 7\dfrac{5}{6} =$

6) $6\dfrac{1}{4} + 1\dfrac{3}{10} =$

B) Subtract these fractions. Give your answers as <u>6 marks</u> mixed numbers if possible.

1) $8\dfrac{7}{10} - 2\dfrac{1}{6} =$

2) $6\dfrac{1}{2} - 5\dfrac{5}{6} =$

3) $2\dfrac{3}{7} - 2\dfrac{3}{10} =$

4) $9\dfrac{1}{3} - 9\dfrac{1}{12} =$

5) $6\dfrac{1}{7} - 3\dfrac{4}{11} =$

6) $6\dfrac{8}{9} - 6\dfrac{4}{7} =$

Score:

Calculate and write your answer in the simplest form. **14 marks**

1) $\dfrac{1}{2} \times \dfrac{2}{4} =$

2) $\dfrac{1}{4} \times \dfrac{2}{5} =$

3) $\dfrac{1}{2} \times \dfrac{1}{2} =$

4) $\dfrac{5}{16} \times \dfrac{1}{2} =$

5) $\dfrac{2}{3} \times \dfrac{5}{10} =$

6) $\dfrac{1}{2} \times \dfrac{1}{5} =$

7) $\dfrac{6}{7} \times \dfrac{6}{32} =$

8) $\dfrac{1}{2} \times \dfrac{6}{16} =$

9) $\dfrac{4}{7} \times \dfrac{8}{12} =$

10) $\dfrac{2}{5} \times \dfrac{3}{7} =$

11) $\dfrac{3}{5} \times \dfrac{2}{4} =$

12) $\dfrac{10}{16} \times \dfrac{1}{7} =$

13) $\dfrac{1}{2} \times \dfrac{2}{5} =$

14) $\dfrac{1}{3} \times \dfrac{12}{14} =$

Score:

# Multiplying Fractions

Calculate and write your answer in the simplest form. **14 marks**

1) $\dfrac{4}{5} \times \dfrac{5}{7} =$

2) $\dfrac{3}{7} \times \dfrac{2}{4} =$

3) $\dfrac{1}{2} \times \dfrac{1}{2} =$

4) $\dfrac{1}{2} \times \dfrac{4}{8} =$

5) $\dfrac{1}{5} \times \dfrac{4}{32} =$

6) $\dfrac{1}{3} \times \dfrac{2}{3} =$

7) $\dfrac{1}{8} \times \dfrac{10}{14} =$

8) $\dfrac{1}{3} \times \dfrac{4}{16} =$

9) $\dfrac{1}{6} \times \dfrac{2}{7} =$

10) $\dfrac{1}{2} \times \dfrac{3}{6} =$

11) $\dfrac{9}{11} \times \dfrac{2}{4} =$

12) $\dfrac{3}{4} \times \dfrac{2}{8} =$

13) $\dfrac{1}{7} \times \dfrac{2}{4} =$

14) $\dfrac{1}{3} \times \dfrac{1}{7} =$

Score:

## Calculate and write your answer in the simplest form. <u>14 marks</u>

1)  $8 \times \dfrac{1}{2} =$

2)  $4 \times \dfrac{6}{11} =$

3)  $6 \times \dfrac{2}{4} =$

4)  $2 \times \dfrac{10}{12} =$

5)  $6 \times \dfrac{4}{14} =$

6)  $8 \times \dfrac{2}{6} =$

7)  $8 \times \dfrac{1}{3} =$

8)  $3 \times \dfrac{6}{9} =$

9)  $4 \times \dfrac{8}{12} =$

10)  $3 \times \dfrac{1}{2} =$

11)  $6 \times \dfrac{2}{4} =$

12)  $6 \times \dfrac{2}{8} =$

13)  $8 \times \dfrac{1}{2} =$

14)  $6 \times \dfrac{12}{14} =$

Score:

Calculate and write your answer in the simplest form. __14 marks__

1)  $\dfrac{6}{7} \times 4 =$

2)  $\dfrac{1}{2} \times 4 =$

3)  $\dfrac{7}{8} \times 9 =$

4)  $\dfrac{2}{5} \times 9 =$

5)  $\dfrac{1}{2} \times 4 =$

6)  $\dfrac{1}{2} \times 7 =$

7)  $\dfrac{1}{2} \times 5 =$

8)  $\dfrac{1}{2} \times 4 =$

9)  $\dfrac{1}{3} \times 3 =$

10) $\dfrac{4}{5} \times 6 =$

11) $\dfrac{1}{3} \times 2 =$

12) $\dfrac{3}{11} \times 6 =$

13) $\dfrac{1}{3} \times 8 =$

14) $\dfrac{1}{2} \times 8 =$

Score:

Calculate and write your answer in the simplest form. **14 marks**

1) $\dfrac{2}{4} \div 3 =$

2) $\dfrac{3}{5} \div 5 =$

3) $\dfrac{5}{7} \div 3 =$

4) $\dfrac{1}{3} \div 9 =$

5) $\dfrac{2}{4} \div 6 =$

6) $\dfrac{4}{7} \div 8 =$

7) $\dfrac{6}{9} \div 7 =$

8) $\dfrac{2}{3} \div 6 =$

9) $\dfrac{3}{6} \div 7 =$

10) $\dfrac{3}{9} \div 8 =$

11) $\dfrac{3}{5} \div 5 =$

12) $\dfrac{1}{2} \div 9 =$

13) $\dfrac{2}{4} \div 8 =$

14) $\dfrac{2}{5} \div 7 =$

Score:

# Dividing Fractions by Whole Numbers

Calculate and write your answer in the simplest form. **14 marks**

1) $\dfrac{2}{4} \div 6 =$

2) $\dfrac{3}{6} \div 1 =$

3) $\dfrac{1}{2} \div 1 =$

4) $\dfrac{6}{16} \div 2 =$

5) $\dfrac{2}{8} \div 1 =$

6) $\dfrac{6}{7} \div 3 =$

7) $\dfrac{7}{14} \div 3 =$

8) $\dfrac{6}{7} \div 9 =$

9) $\dfrac{28}{32} \div 2 =$

10) $\dfrac{3}{5} \div 6 =$

11) $\dfrac{4}{8} \div 3 =$

12) $\dfrac{14}{16} \div 3 =$

13) $\dfrac{6}{9} \div 2 =$

14) $\dfrac{1}{3} \div 7 =$

Score:

# Multiplying or Dividing by 10, 100 or , 1000

## A) Multiply these numbers.                                8 marks

1) $2.6 \times 10 =$ _____   2) $62.7 \times 10 =$ _____

3) $68.8 \times 100 =$ _____   4) $9.6 \times 10 =$ _____

5) $8.2 \times 10 =$ _____   6) $0.53 \times 1,000 =$ _____

7) $0.72 \times 100 =$ _____   8) $9.6 \times 100 =$ _____

## B) Divide these numbers.                                  8 marks

1) $38,887 \div 1,000 =$ _____   2) $5,735 \div 1,000 =$ _____

3) $69 \div 10 =$ _____   4) $83,676 \div 100 =$ _____

5) $848 \div 100 =$ _____   6) $430 \div 100 =$ _____

7) $64,740 \div 10 =$ _____   8) $41 \div 1,000 =$ _____

Score: ____

# Multiplying or Dividing by 10, 100 or , 1000

## A) Multiply these numbers.                                          <u>8 marks</u>

1)   $1.06 \times 1{,}000 = $ _____      2)   $4.6 \times 10 = $ _____

3)   $5.40 \times 10 = $ _____      4)   $4.3 \times 100 = $ _____

5)   $9.0 \times 100 = $ _____      6)   $33.8 \times 10 = $ _____

7)   $9.18 \times 10 = $ _____      8)   $0.45 \times 100 = $ _____

## B) Divide these numbers.                                          <u>8 marks</u>

1)   $68 \div 1{,}000 = $ _____      2)   $76 \div 10 = $ _____

3)   $92.2 \div 100 = $ _____      4)   $29 \div 1{,}000 = $ _____

5)   $812 \div 1{,}000 = $ _____      6)   $69.2 \div 1{,}000 = $ _____

7)   $93.8 \div 1{,}000 = $ _____      8)   $2{,}139 \div 100 = $ _____

Score:

# Multiplying with Decimals

Multiply.                                                          <u>**16 marks**</u>

1)      6
   × 0.06

2)     47
   × 0.6

3)     63
   × 0.7

4)    781
   × 1.7

5)    129
   × 0.52

6)      4
   × 0.42

7)    178
   × 0.40

8)      8
   × 5.5

9)     76
   × 0.2

10)    611
    × 0.54

11)    72
    × 6.2

12)     5
    × 0.05

13)     4
    × 0.8

14)     8
    × 0.7

15)    812
    × 5.3

16)    91
    × 5.2

Score: [        ]

# Multiplying with Decimals

Multiply.

1)
$$\begin{array}{r} 93 \\ \times\ 0.2 \\ \hline \end{array}$$

2)
$$\begin{array}{r} 38 \\ \times\ 0.45 \\ \hline \end{array}$$

3)
$$\begin{array}{r} 4 \\ \times\ 0.3 \\ \hline \end{array}$$

4)
$$\begin{array}{r} 6 \\ \times\ 0.27 \\ \hline \end{array}$$

5)
$$\begin{array}{r} 8 \\ \times\ 4.2 \\ \hline \end{array}$$

6)
$$\begin{array}{r} 3 \\ \times\ 0.06 \\ \hline \end{array}$$

7)
$$\begin{array}{r} 8 \\ \times\ 0.5 \\ \hline \end{array}$$

8)
$$\begin{array}{r} 18 \\ \times\ 0.05 \\ \hline \end{array}$$

9)
$$\begin{array}{r} 835 \\ \times\ 0.7 \\ \hline \end{array}$$

10)
$$\begin{array}{r} 5 \\ \times\ 0.03 \\ \hline \end{array}$$

11)
$$\begin{array}{r} 8 \\ \times\ 0.41 \\ \hline \end{array}$$

12)
$$\begin{array}{r} 604 \\ \times\ 0.09 \\ \hline \end{array}$$

13)
$$\begin{array}{r} 8 \\ \times\ 0.4 \\ \hline \end{array}$$

14)
$$\begin{array}{r} 934 \\ \times\ 0.6 \\ \hline \end{array}$$

15)
$$\begin{array}{r} 538 \\ \times\ 0.61 \\ \hline \end{array}$$

16)
$$\begin{array}{r} 3 \\ \times\ 0.31 \\ \hline \end{array}$$

Score:

Multiply.                                                            <u>16 marks</u>

1)      0.08
   ×    26

2)      2.1
   ×    84

3)      7.2
   ×   833

4)      0.24
   ×    31

5)      0.07
   ×    99

6)      0.03
   ×   482

7)      0.74
   ×   251

8)      0.5
   ×   443

9)      5.6
   ×    60

10)     0.7
   ×   887

11)     0.16
   ×   330

12)     5.1
   ×   357

13)     0.05
   ×    89

14)     2.1
   ×    35

15)     0.06
   ×    21

16)     0.03
   ×   146

Score:

# Multiplying with Decimals

Multiply.

1)    0.03
  ×  400

2)    0.3
  ×  74

3)    0.06
  ×  55

4)    0.07
  ×  629

5)    0.05
  ×  28

6)    0.2
  ×  24

7)    0.56
  ×  88

8)    9.5
  ×  12

9)    7.7
  ×  34

10)    0.5
  ×  415

11)    0.18
  ×  453

12)    0.79
  ×  788

13)    0.9
  ×  98

14)    4.1
  ×  237

15)    5.8
  ×  72

16)    0.49
  ×  39

Score:

# Dividing with Decimals

Use the written method to calculate these problems. **9 marks**

1)

$5\overline{)164}$

2)

$6\overline{)696}$

3)

$3\overline{)857}$

4)

$6\overline{)813}$

5)

$9\overline{)909}$

6)

$5\overline{)452}$

7)

$5\overline{)736}$

8)

$7\overline{)732}$

9)

$8\overline{)997}$

Score:

# Dividing with Decimals

Use the written method to calculate these problems. <u>9 marks</u>

1)

$4\overline{)218}$

2)

$7\overline{)411}$

3)

$3\overline{)584}$

4)

$8\overline{)692}$

5)

$6\overline{)508}$

6)

$3\overline{)731}$

7)

$3\overline{)335}$

8)

$5\overline{)591}$

9)

$9\overline{)735}$

Score:

# Dividing with Decimals

Use the written method to calculate these problems. **9 marks**

1) $6\overline{)2.98}$

2) $6\overline{)57.8}$

3) $3\overline{)19.5}$

4) $5\overline{)68.6}$

5) $2\overline{)2.28}$

6) $6\overline{)65.8}$

7) $7\overline{)2.04}$

8) $6\overline{)95.9}$

9) $5\overline{)5.25}$

Score:

# Dividing with Decimals

Use the written method to calculate these problems. **9 marks**

1) $5\overline{)53.7}$

2) $5\overline{)67.9}$

3) $7\overline{)6.84}$

4) $8\overline{)2.42}$

5) $6\overline{)15.8}$

6) $6\overline{)5.19}$

7) $8\overline{)5.92}$

8) $5\overline{)69.8}$

9) $2\overline{)7.80}$

Score:

# Rounding Decimals

Round each decimal to the underlined place value.

1)   0.9<u>2</u>6 = _____

2)   0.0<u>4</u>9 = _____

3)   8.<u>2</u> = _____

4)   <u>0</u>.885 = _____

5)   99.<u>3</u> = _____

6)   0.6<u>2</u>1 = _____

7)   3.7<u>3</u> = _____

8)   6.4<u>3</u> = _____

9)   <u>7</u>.5 = _____

10)  3.<u>2</u> = _____

11)  <u>1</u>.8 = _____

12)  3.5<u>4</u> = _____

13)  <u>0</u>.914 = _____

14)  3<u>6</u>.7 = _____

15)  0.<u>0</u>11 = _____

16)  0.9<u>8</u>4 = _____

17)  <u>0</u>.690 = _____

18)  <u>2</u>.25 = _____

19)  0.<u>7</u>3 = _____

20)  0.<u>2</u>90 = _____

Score: [    ]

Round each decimal to the underlined place value.     <u>20 marks</u>

1)   0.7_7 = _____

2)   3.2_7 = _____

3)   _9.57 = _____

4)   1_6.8 = _____

5)   71._1 = _____

6)   _0.466 = _____

7)   0.2_50 = _____

8)   0._220 = _____

9)   _0.421 = _____

10)  0._543 = _____

11)  _0.29 = _____

12)  0.8_7 = _____

13)  _1.1 = _____

14)  _6.04 = _____

15)  5._65 = _____

16)  0._047 = _____

17)  18._4 = _____

18)  0._373 = _____

19)  _0.082 = _____

20)  0.0_38 = _____

Score: [        ]

# Fractions, Decimals & Percentages

## A) Convert the following fractions into decimals.  <u>12 marks</u>

1) $\dfrac{1}{2}$ =

2) $\dfrac{53}{100}$ =

3) $\dfrac{8}{10}$ =

4) $\dfrac{1}{20}$ =

5) $\dfrac{27}{50}$ =

6) $\dfrac{457}{1000}$ =

7) $\dfrac{14}{20}$ =

8) $\dfrac{21}{50}$ =

9) $\dfrac{69}{100}$ =

10) $\dfrac{9}{10}$ =

11) $\dfrac{80}{1000}$ =

12) $\dfrac{3}{20}$ =

## B) Convert the following decimals into fractions.  <u>8 marks</u>

1) 0.3 =

2) 0.16 =

3) 0.5 =

4) 0.1 =

5) 0.4 =

6) 0.6 =

7) 0.09 =

8) 0.8 =

Score:

# Fractions, Decimals & Percentages

A) Convert the following fractions into decimals.    <u>8 marks</u>

1)  $\dfrac{8}{9}$ =

2)  $\dfrac{8}{12}$ =

3)  $\dfrac{3}{100}$ =

4)  $\dfrac{2}{4}$ =

5)  $\dfrac{717}{1000}$ =

6)  $\dfrac{16}{20}$ =

7)  $\dfrac{4}{10}$ =

8)  $\dfrac{1}{2}$ =

B) Convert the following decimals into fractions.    <u>12 marks</u>

1)  0.8 =

2)  0.286 =

3)  0.667 =

4)  0.5 =

5)  0.74 =

6)  0.44 =

7)  0.4 =

8)  0.125 =

9)  0.333 =

10)  0.444 =

11)  0.75 =

12)  0.167 =

Score:

# Fractions, Decimals & Percentages

## A) Write each of these decimals as a percentage.   12 marks

1) $0.33 =$

2) $0.71 =$

3) $0.69 =$

4) $0.13 =$

5) $0.43 =$

6) $0.89 =$

7) $0.62 =$

8) $0.1 =$

9) $0.61 =$

10) $0.57 =$

11) $0.99 =$

12) $0.79 =$

## B) Write each of these percentages as a decimal.   8 marks

1) $49\% =$

2) $91\% =$

3) $40\% =$

4) $97\% =$

5) $18\% =$

6) $56\% =$

7) $51\% =$

8) $35\% =$

Score:

# Fractions, Decimals & Percentages

A) Write each of these decimals as a percentage.     <u>**8 marks**</u>

1)   0.93 =

2)   0.17 =

3)   0.1 =

4)   0.9 =

5)   0.33 =

6)   0.04 =

7)   0.28 =

8)   0.41 =

B) Write each of these percentages as a decimal.     <u>**12 marks**</u>

1)   95 % =

2)   48 % =

3)   63 % =

4)   31 % =

5)   39 % =

6)   76 % =

7)   2 % =

8)   9 % =

9)   67 % =

10)   93 % =

11)   25 % =

12)   78 % =

Score:

A) Peanuts cost 60p for 100 grams.                                    <u>1 mark</u>

What is the cost of 350 grams of peanuts?

_____

B) Dexter is making some peanut butter cookies.

He has this list of ingredients to make 8 biscuits.

**Peanut butter cookies (Makes 8)**

125 g peanut butter

70 g sugar

1 large egg

1 teaspoon vanilla

1) How much of each ingredient does Dexter need to    <u>4 marks</u>

make 24 biscuits?

Peanut butter [          g ]          Sugar [          g ]

Large egg [          ]          teaspoon vanilla [          ]

2) Mariam only has 62.5g of peanut butter to make          <u>1 mark</u>

some cookies. What is the maximum number of cookies

he can make? _____

_____

Score: [          ]

A) Amira buys 3 cans of water for $15.

1) How much do 6 cans cost? _____ 1 mark

_____

2) How much do 9 cans cost? _____ 1 mark

_____

3) How much do 12 cans cost? _____ 1 mark

_____

B) The cost of eight ice creams is $24.

Calculate the cost of three ice creams. 1 mark

_____

_____

C) A simple recipe needs 150 g of flour and 60 g butter.

If 375 g of flour is used, how much butter is needed? 1 mark

_____

_____

D) 100g of cheese costs 50p.

Layla buys 250g of the cheese.

How much does she pay? 1 mark

_____

_____

Score:

Identify the scale factor that been used to enlarge these shapes:     <u>2 marks</u>

1)

2)

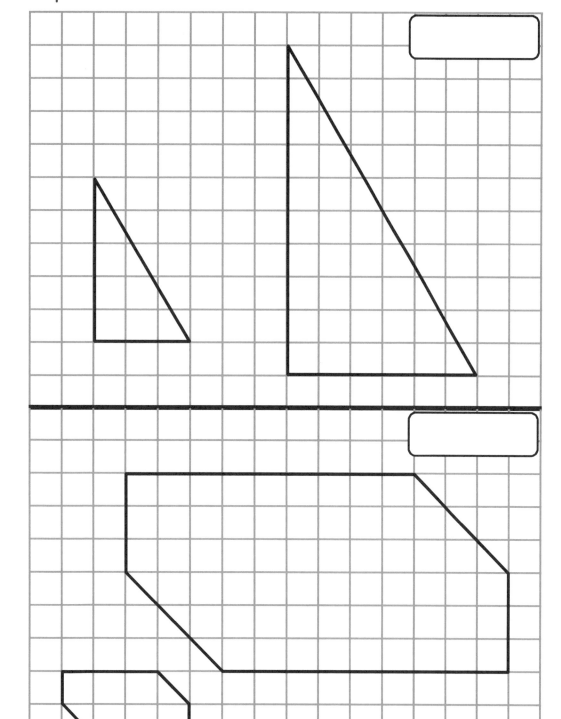

Score:

Identify the scale factor that been used to enlarge these shapes:    2 marks

1)

2)

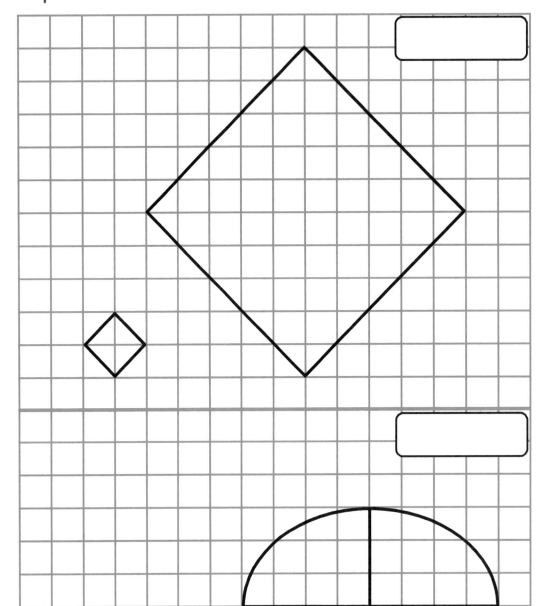

Score:

The shaded shape is translated from A to B and enlarged by a scale factor of 4.
Draw the enlarged shape on the grid.

**2 marks**

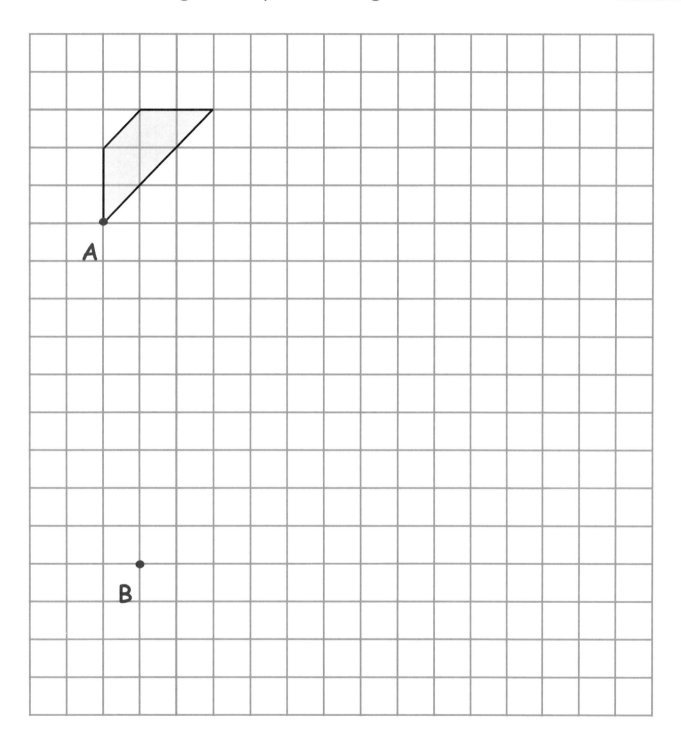

Score:

The shaded shape is translated from A to B and enlarged by a scale factor of 3.
Draw the enlarged shape on the grid.

**2 marks**

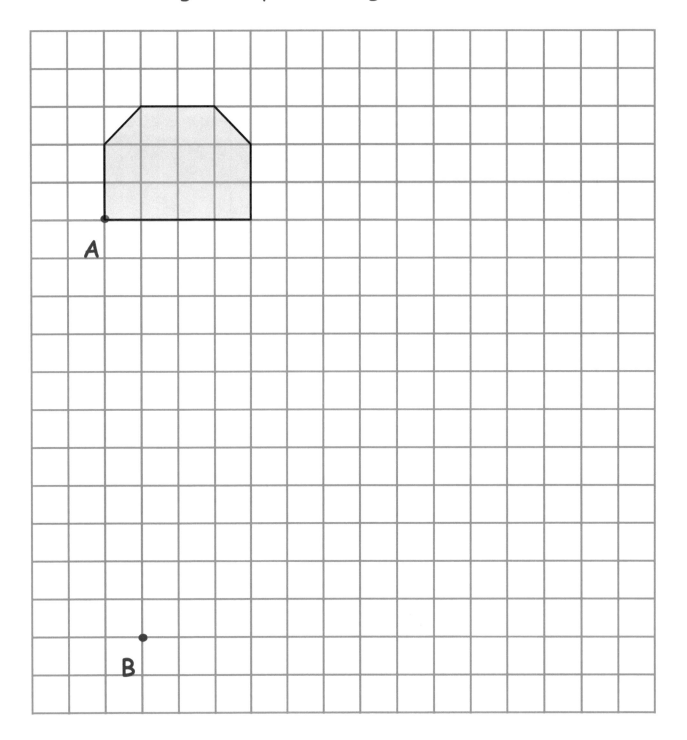

Score:

# Percentages of Amounts

A) Calculate these percentages.                    5 marks

1)      10% of 110 = _____

2)      50% of 230 = _____

3)      70% of 30 = _____

4)      90% of 40 = _____

5)      75% of 216 = _____

B) Calculate these percentages.                    5 marks

1)      75% of $61.00 = _____

2)      15% of $71.00 = _____

3)      70% of $101.00 = _____

4)      10% of $192.00 = _____

5)      20% of $80.00 = _____

Score: [          ]

A) Create a pie chart to show children's favourite fruits:

**38% ananas, 26% strawberry, 19% apple, 17% banana.**

Find 38%, 26%, 19%, 17% of 360 and measure

accordingly.                                                            <u>4 marks</u>

B) In a survey, some people were asked to name their

favourite animal.

| Animals | Number of people |
|---------|------------------|
| Dogs | 40% |
| Cats | 30% |
| Chickens | 10% |
| Horses | 20% |

If you were to draw a pie chart to show this information,
what size angle would be needed to show the percentage
answer for chickens and dogs?                              <u>2 marks</u>

chickens [          ]                    dogs [          ]

Score: [          ]

A) Mourad planted some seeds. For every 5 seeds Mourad planted, only 3 seeds grew. Altogether, 18 seeds grew. How many seeds did Mourad plant?                    **2 marks**

B) In a class of 20 children, 15 children are girls and the rest are boys.

What is the ratio of girls to boys?                    **2 marks**

C) In a class 3/5 of the students are girls.

If there are 120 students in total, how many girls are there?                    **2 marks**

Score:

A) A book has 120 pages divided into 8 equal chapters. Olivia has read 3/8 of the book, and Harrison has read 45 pages. Explain why Olivia and Harrison have read the same amount of the book?

2 marks

B) On the farm, 1 in 6 animals is a goat.

2 marks

If there are 180 animals in total, how many goats are there?

C) Harry is making a fish pie.

The recipe says that for every three potatoes he uses, he needs 290 grams of fish.

If he uses 870 grams of fish, how many potatoes will he need?

2 marks

Score:

Calculate the value of the variable in each equation.  <u>10 marks</u>

1)  $10a - 12 = 188$ _____

2)  $15 + 7a = 92$ _____

3)  $3a - 4 = 53$ _____

4)  $113 = 13 + 10a$ _____

5)  $238 = 18a - 14$ _____

6)  $324 = 18a$ _____

7)  $85 = 17a$ _____

8)  $346 = 4 + 18a$ _____

9)  $4a - 5 = 23$ _____

10)  $88 = 11a$ _____

Score: _____

# Simple Formulae

Calculate the value of the variable in each equation.   **10 marks**

1) $6 + 11a = 193$ _____

2) $10 = 5a$ _____

3) $15a - 9 = 201$ _____

4) $5a - 17 = 18$ _____

5) $224 = 19a - 4$ _____

6) $16a - 20 = 268$ _____

7) $14a = 252$ _____

8) $120 = 6a$ _____

9) $19 + 10a = 169$ _____

10) $64 = 16a$ _____

Score: _____

# Simple Formulae

A) Calculate the value of each expression. b = 4.   **6 marks**

1)   $11 + b =$ _____

2)   $b - 26 =$ _____

3)   $27 + b =$ _____

4)   $3 + b =$ _____

5)   $13 + b =$ _____

6)   $13b + 29 =$ _____

B) Calculate the value of each expression. b = 14   **4 marks**

1)   $10b + 15 =$ _____

2)   $b + 15 =$ _____

3)   $29 + 12b =$ _____

4)   $b + 12 =$ _____

Score: [____]

# Simple Formulae

Calculate the value of each expression. b = 5.          <u>10 marks</u>

1)   3n – n = _____

2)   6(7 + n) = _____

3)   3(7 – n) = _____

4)   12(8 + n) = _____

5)   6 + (n + 5) – 10 + (3n) = ____

6)   12(4 – n) = _____

7)   10 + (3n + 3) = _____

8)   6 + (7n + 7) = _____

9)   5 + (5n + 11) = _____

10)   11(3 – n) = _____

Score: _____

# Sequences

A) Find the missing numbers in these sequences.    <u>10 marks</u>

1)

| 6 | 11 |  | 21 |  | 31 |  |  |  |
|---|----|--|----|--|----|--|--|--|

2)

|  |  | 32 | 40 |  | 56 | 64 |  |  |
|--|--|----|----|--|----|----|--|--|

B) Fill in the empty blanks. Write a rule to represent the relationship between input and output.    <u>12 marks</u>

1)

| Input | Output |
|-------|--------|
| 56    | 1,400  |
| 7     | 175    |
| 51    |        |
| 36    |        |

_____

2)

| Input | Output |
|-------|--------|
| 702   | 18     |
| 663   | 17     |
| 1,833 |        |
| 1,248 |        |

_____

3)

| Input | Output |
|-------|--------|
| 9     | 378    |
| 48    | 2,016  |
| 52    |        |
| 44    |        |

_____

4)

| Input | Output |
|-------|--------|
| 39    | 468    |
| 6     | 72     |
| 26    |        |
| 14    |        |

_____

Score: [____]

A) Complete the table for the given function machine. <u>8 marks</u>

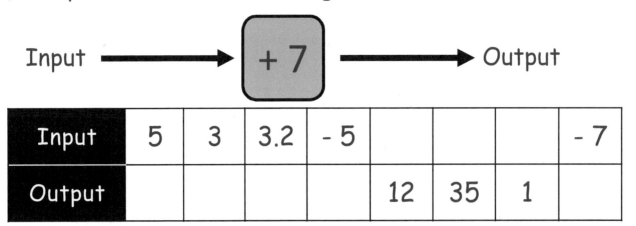

| Input | 5 | 3 | 3.2 | - 5 | | | | - 7 |
|---|---|---|---|---|---|---|---|---|
| Output | | | | | 12 | 35 | 1 | |

B) Dexter draws a function machine. It doubles a number and then subtracts 4. Dexter sees that one of the outputs is 16.

1) What was the input? <u>1 mark</u>

Then dexter inputs 22.

2) What output will Dexter see? <u>1 mark</u>

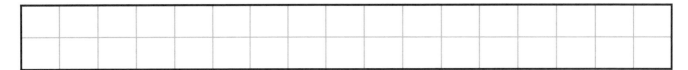

3) Write the formula for Dexter's machine. <u>1 mark</u>

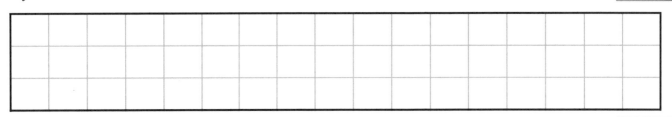

Score:

A) Daisy and Rosie are sisters. This formula can be used to calculate Daisy's age, compared to Rosie's age:

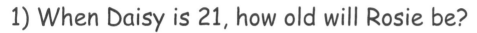

$$d + 7 = r$$

❖ **d** stands for Daisy's age.

❖ **r** stands for Rosie's age.

1) When Daisy is 21, how old will Rosie be?

2) When Rosie is 33, how old will Daisy be?

B) What is the total of the angles inside a quadrilateral?

How can we find b?

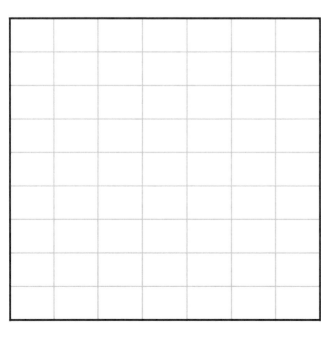

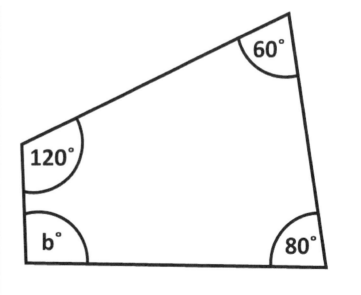

Score:

A) Simplify these formulas.                                    <u>8 marks</u>

1) $-6y - 8 - 3 - 6y$                    2) $7 - 5(2y - 5)$

_____                    _____

_____                    _____

_____                    _____

3) $3 + 9y - 4 + 9y - 2 + 6y$            4) $4y - 9y + 2y - 7 + 2$

_____                    _____

_____                    _____

_____                    _____

B) For each question, **choose** the expression that matches one of the problems algebraically, and then **solve** the problem.                                    <u>6 marks</u>

1) A number has thirteen added to it to make 42. What is the number?

   $13+y=42$        $42=y-13$        $y=13+42$        $y=$ _____

2) What number has 12 added to it to make 37?

   $y-12=37$        $12+y=37$        $y+12=37$        $y=$ _____

3) Fourteen is subtracted from a number to make 22. What is the number?

   $22-y=14$        $14-y=22$        $y-14=22$        $y=$ _____

Score: [        ]

A) Look at this equation.

$$3a + b = 10$$

*a* and *b* are both positive whole numbers and are both greater than zero.

Write all possible values of *b*.                    <u>3 marks</u>

_____

_____

_____

_____

B) Which pair of values does not satisfy the equation?  <u>1 mark</u>

$$a \div b = 3$$

| a = 18 | a = 12 | a = 16 |
| b = 6  | b = 4  | b = 4  |

C) Find 3 different possible pairs of values for **X** and **Y** in this equation:                    <u>3 marks</u>

$$XY = 24$$

_____

_____

_____

_____

Score: [    ]

A) Find out the value of both symbols.  2 marks

$$7 \times \text{♥} + 14 = 70$$

$$32 \div (8 - \text{☺}) = 8$$

 _____

 _____

B) X and Y are whole numbers that satisfy the equation:

$$X + 2Y = 52$$

### *True or False?*  4 marks

1) X must be an even number. _____

2) Y must be an odd number. _____

3) Y can be even or odd. _____

4) X can be even or odd. _____

C) Use this equation to fill in the missing information in the

table below.  4 marks

$$5c - 8 = d$$

| Value of c | Value of d |
|:----------:|:----------:|
| 5 | |
| | 2 |
| 7 | |
| | 12 |

Score: ____

# Units

## A) Convert the given measures to the new units.          8 marks

1)  18 L = _____ mL    2)  60 km = _____ m

3)  48 g = _____ kg    4)  19 km = _____ m

5)  56 g = _____ kg    6)  68 kg = _____ g

7)  30 L = _____ mL    8)  45 mL = _____ L


## B) Convert the given measures of time to alternate          8 marks
measures of time.

1)  14 yr = _____ wk    2)  27 sec = _____ sec

3)  23 min = _____ min    4)  18 wk = _____ dy

5)  16 sec = _____ hr    6)  19 min = _____ sec

7)  28 dy = _____ hr    8)  20 hr = _____ dy

Score: [         ]

# Units

## A) Convert the given measures to the new units. 8 marks

1)   51 cm = _____ m

2)  71 cm = _____ m

3)   24 g = _____ kg

4)  52 g = _____ kg

5)   74 cm = _____ mm

6)  45 cm = _____ mm

7)   40 g = _____ kg

8)  72 cm = _____ mm

## B) Convert the given measures of time to alternate measures of time. 8 marks

1)   25 hr = _____ min

2)  15 sec = _____ min

3)   11 hr = _____ dy

4)  22 min = _____ sec

5)   15 dy = _____ hr

6)  21 yr = _____ wk

7)   23 dy = _____ wk

8)  10 yr = _____ dy

Score: _____

A) Convert from miles to kilometres.                    **6 marks**

1)  1 mi = _____ km    2)  123 mi = _____ km

3)  488 mi = _____ km    4)  209 mi = _____ km

5)  325 mi = _____ km    6)  427 mi = _____ km


B) Convert from kilometres to miles.                    **6 marks**

1)  128 km = _____ mi    2)  431 km = _____ mi

3)  106 km = _____ mi    4)  66 km = _____ mi

5)  180 km = _____ mi    6)  207 km = _____ mi


C) Convert the given measures of time to alternate       **6 marks**
measures of time.

1)  14 dy = _____ hr    2)  10 hr = _____ dy

3)  17 yr = _____ dy    4)  15 min = _____ hr

5)  14 yr = _____ wk    6)  19 sec = _____ min


Score: [        ]

A) Convert the given measures of time to alternate measures of time.    **6 marks**

1)    23 yr = _____ wk

2) 19 dy = _____ wk

3)    20 yr = _____ dy

4) 21 sec = _____ hr

5)    26 sec = _____ min

6) 23 hr = _____ min

B) Convert from miles to kilometres.    **6 marks**

1)    52 mi = _____ km

2) 394 mi = _____ km

3)    71 mi = _____ km

4) 193 mi = _____ km

5)    203 mi = _____ km

6) 180 mi = _____ km

C) Convert from kilometres to miles.    **6 marks**

1)    84 km = _____ mi

2) 491 km = _____ mi

3)    60 km = _____ mi

4) 418 km = _____ mi

5)    61 km = _____ mi

6) 277 km = _____ mi

Score: [      ]

Find the area of these triangles.

1)

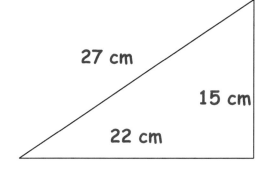

_____

2)

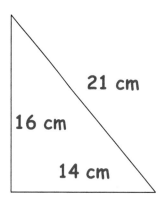

_____

3)

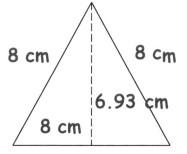

_____

4)

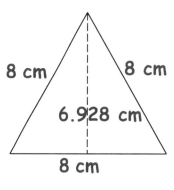

_____

5)

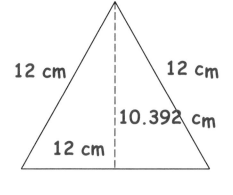

_____

6)

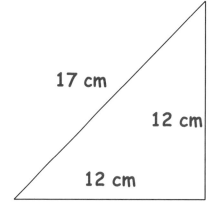

_____

Score:

Find the area of these triangles.

1)
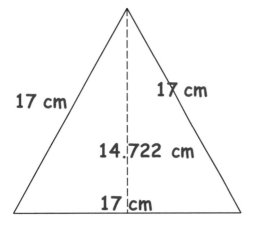

17 cm    17 cm

14.722 cm

17 cm

_____

2)
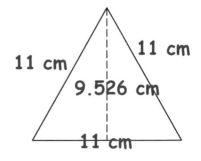

11 cm    11 cm

9.526 cm

11 cm

_____

3)
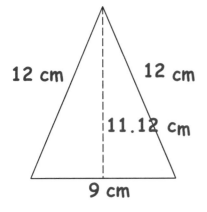

12 cm    12 cm

11.12 cm

9 cm

_____

4)
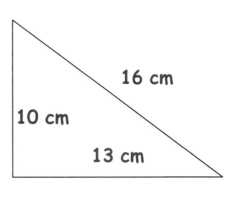

16 cm

10 cm

13 cm

_____

5)
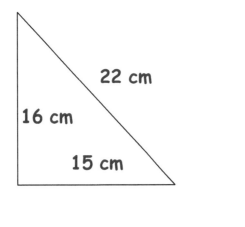

22 cm

16 cm

15 cm

_____

6)
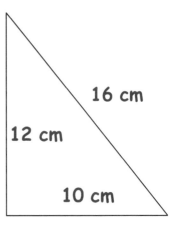

16 cm

12 cm

10 cm

_____

Score: [    ]

Find the area of these parallelograms.

1)
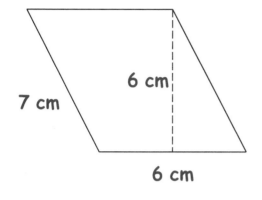

_____

2)
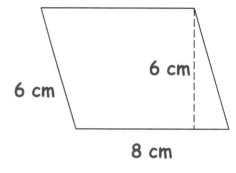

_____

3)
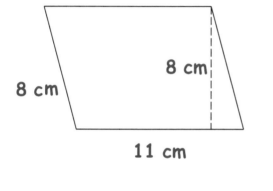

_____

4)
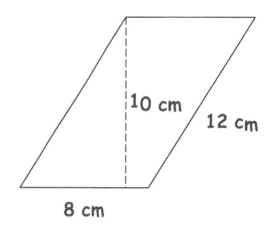

_____

5)
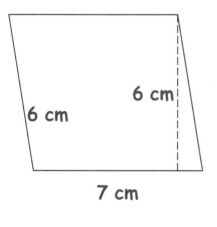

_____

6)
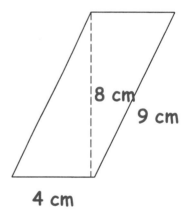

_____

Score: _____

Find the area of these parallelograms.

1)
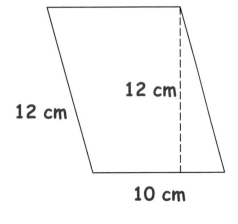

12 cm   12 cm

12 cm

10 cm

_____

2)
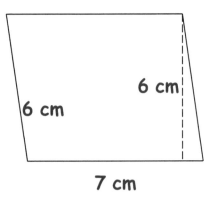

6 cm   6 cm

7 cm

_____

3)
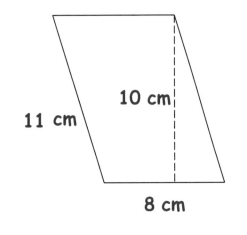

10 cm

11 cm

8 cm

_____

4)
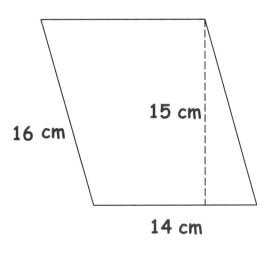

15 cm

16 cm

14 cm

_____

5)
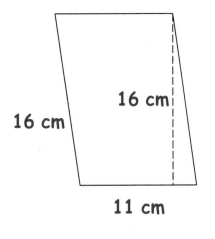

16 cm

16 cm

11 cm

_____

6)
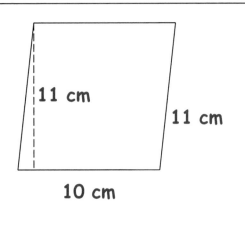

11 cm   11 cm

10 cm

_____

Score: ☐

Find the area and perimeter of these shapes.

1)

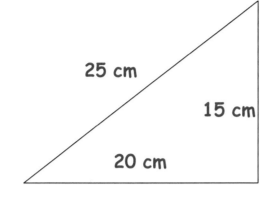

_____

2)

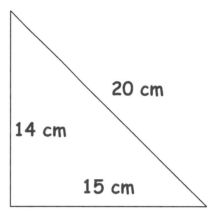

_____

3)

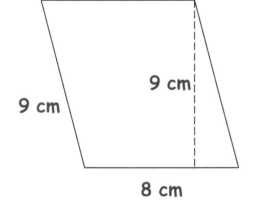

_____

4)

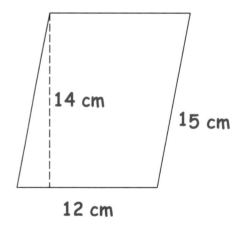

_____

Score: ____

Find the area and perimeter of these shapes.   4 marks

1)
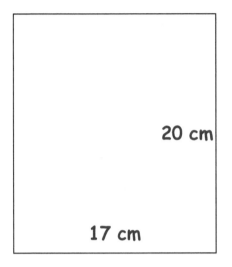

20 cm

17 cm

_____

2)
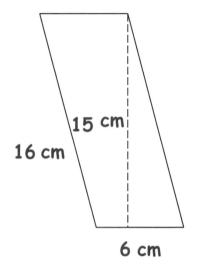

15 cm

16 cm

6 cm

_____

3)
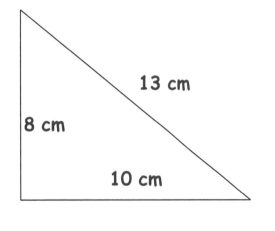

13 cm

8 cm

10 cm

_____

4)
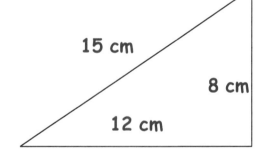

15 cm

8 cm

12 cm

_____

Score:

If each cube has a volume of 1 cm³, find the volume **6 marks** of each solid.

1)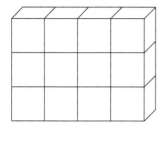

_____

2)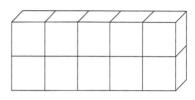

_____

3)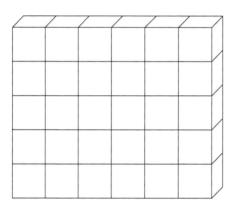

_____

4)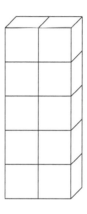

_____

5)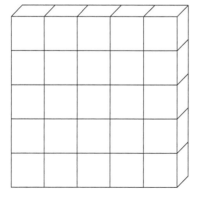

_____

6)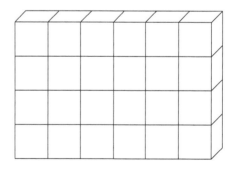

_____

Score: [ ]

If each cube has a volume of 1 cm³, find the volume of each solid.

1)

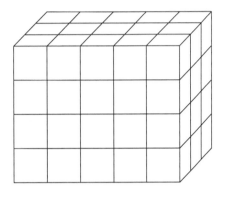

_____

2)

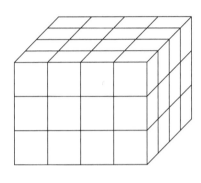

_____

3)

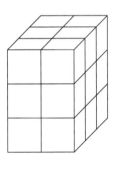

_____

4)

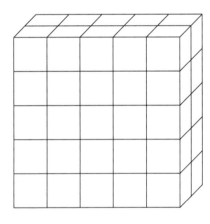

_____

5)

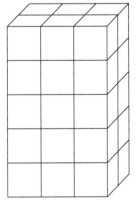

_____

6)

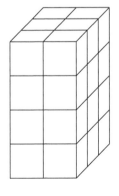

_____

Score: [    ]

If each cube has a volume of 1 cm³, find the volume **6 marks** of each solid.

1)

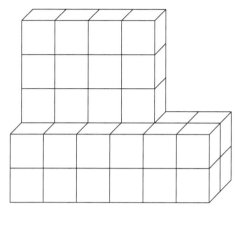

_____

2)

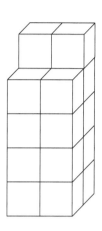

_____

3)

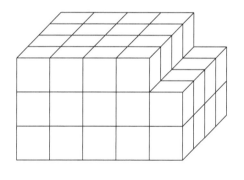

_____

4)

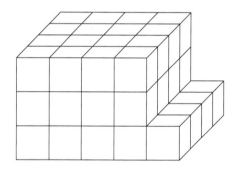

_____

5)

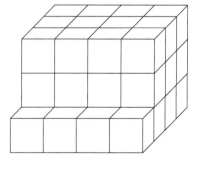

_____

6)

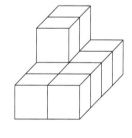

_____

Score: [     ]

If each cube has a volume of 1 cm³, find the volume of each solid.    **6 marks**

1)

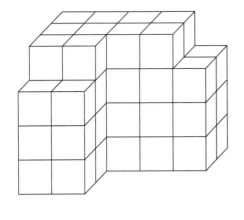

_____

2)

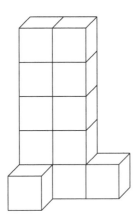

_____

3)

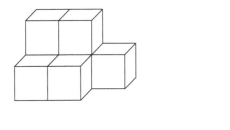

_____

4)

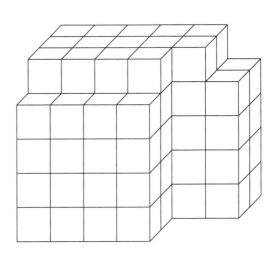

_____

5)

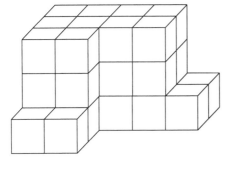

_____

6)

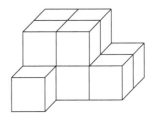

_____

Score: [     ]

Calculate the volume of these cuboids. **4 marks**

1)

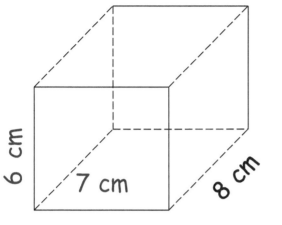

_____

2)

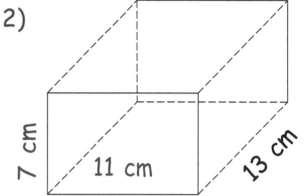

_____

3)

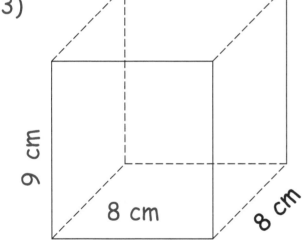

_____

4)

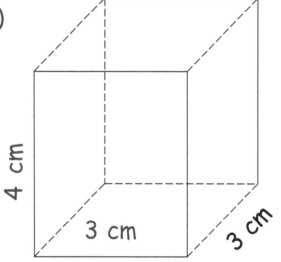

_____

Score: [     ]

Calculate the volume of these cuboids.

1)

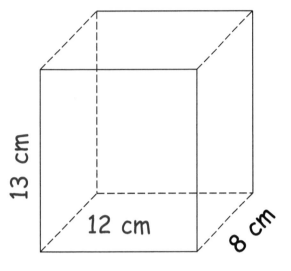

2)

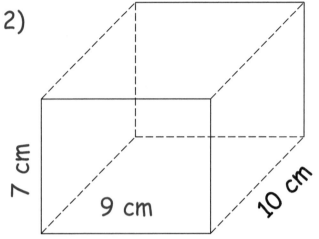

_____

_____

3)

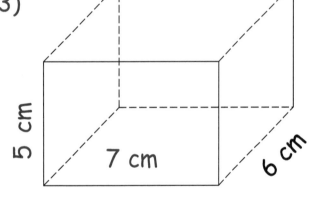

4)

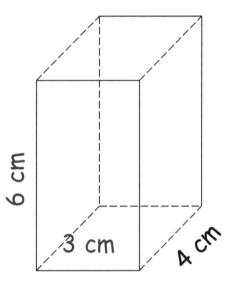

_____

_____

Score: [          ]

Calculate the volume of these cuboids.                     <u>4 marks</u>

1)
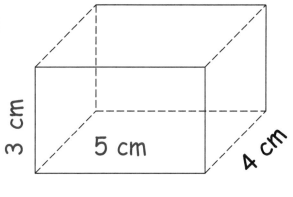

2)
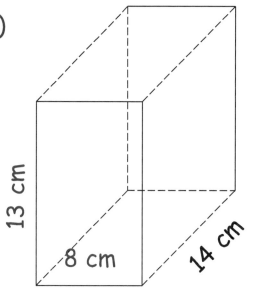

3)
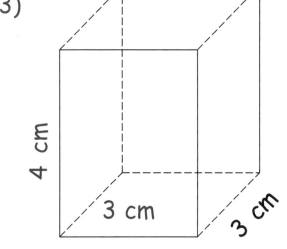

4)
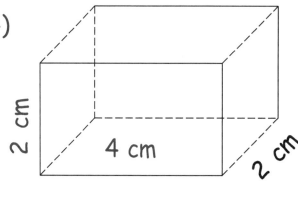

Score:

A) Use the symbols < > or = to compare the volume of each pair of cubes / cuboids (these shapes are not to scale). **4 marks**

| Shape 1 | < > or = | Shape 2 |
|---|---|---|
| 7 cm, 5 cm, 5 cm | | 10 cm, 6 cm, 7 cm |
| 6 cm, 9 cm, 8 cm | | 2 cm, 2 cm, 4 cm |
| 4 cm, 8 cm, 4 cm | | 4 cm, 16 cm, 2 cm |
| 13 cm, 17 cm, 13 cm | | 22 cm, 33 cm, 21 cm |

Score:

A) On the grid, draw a hexagon that has more than 3 right-angles.

1 mark

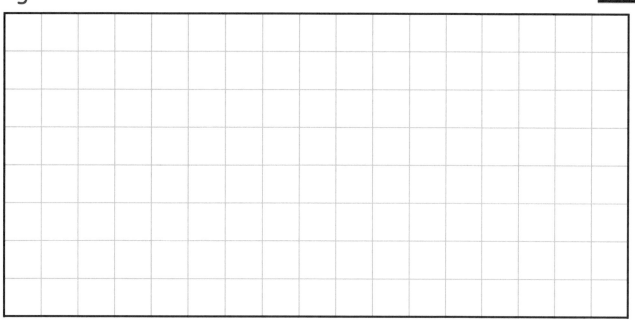

B) Draw a scale drawing of this triangle.

Remember to work carefully and measure the lengths and angles accurately.

1 mark

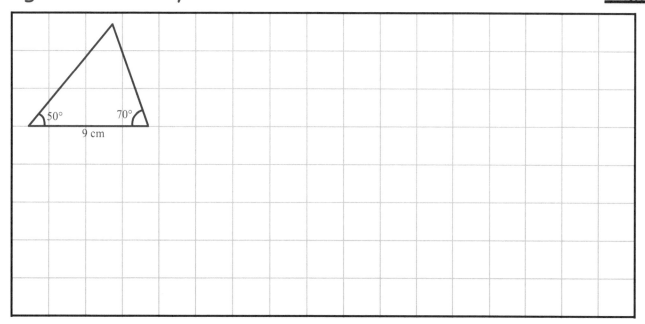

Score:

A) Draw the quadrilateral. Then measure the angles at A and B and the length of AB.    <u>1 mark</u>

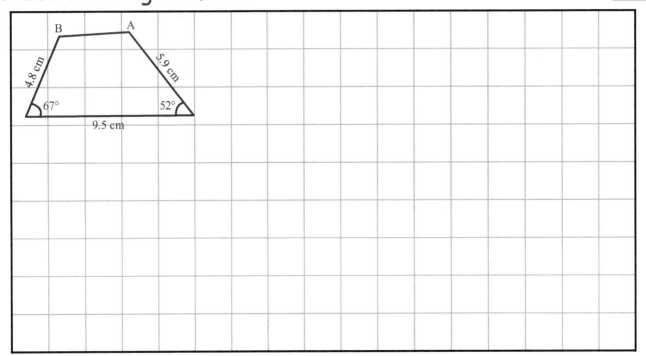

A) Can you draw this shape to scale with a ruler?    <u>1 mark</u>

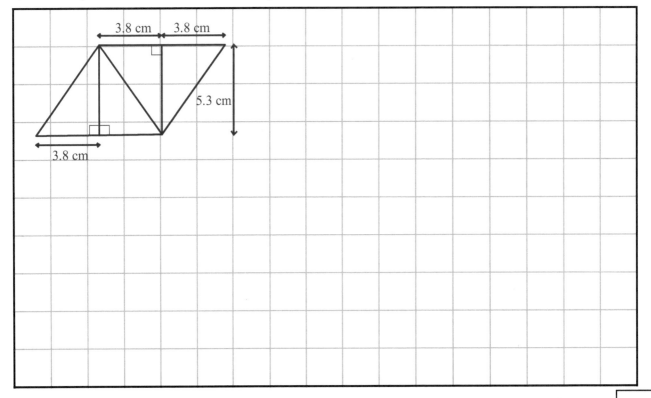

Score:

A) Can you draw a right-angled triangle with lengths of 5cm and 12cm and angles of 90° and 23°.

Work out the last length the missing angle.       <u>1 mark</u>

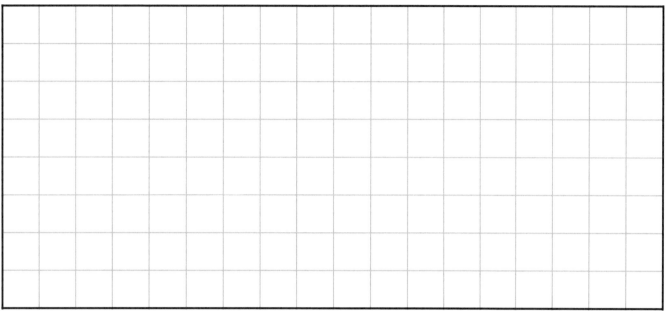

B) Draw a parallelogram, where each edge measures 4cm, two internal angles each measure 100° and two internal angles each measure 80°.       <u>1 mark</u>

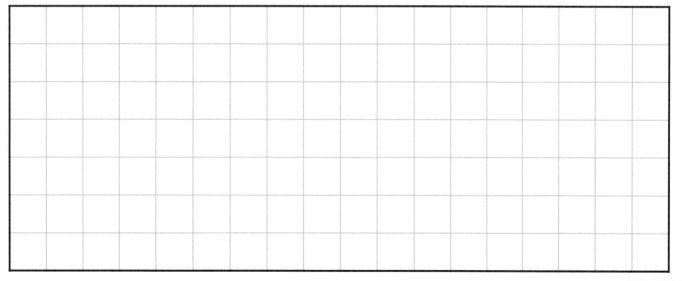

Score:

A) Describe the properties of these 3D shapes.    <u>20 marks</u>

| Name | Number of Faces | Number of Edges | Number of Vertices | number of curved faces |
|---|---|---|---|---|
| Cuboid | | | | |
| Triangular Prism | | | | |
| Pentagonal Prism | | | | |
| Triangular Pyramid | | | | |
| Hexagonal Prism | | | | |

B) Name these shapes.    <u>4 marks</u>

| Properties | Name of shape |
|---|---|
| 5 vertices and 5 faces. | |
| 0 flat faces, 1 curved face, 0 edges, 0 vertices. | |
| 2 flat faces, 1 curved face, 2 edges, 0 vertices. | |
| 1 flat face, 1 curved face, 1 edge, 1 vertex. | |

C) A 3D shape has 8 vertices, 6 faces. All the faces have equal dimensions. Put a ring around the correct name for this 3-D shape.

<u>1 mark</u>

rectangle            pyramid            cube


cylinder            square

Score:

Name these shapes.

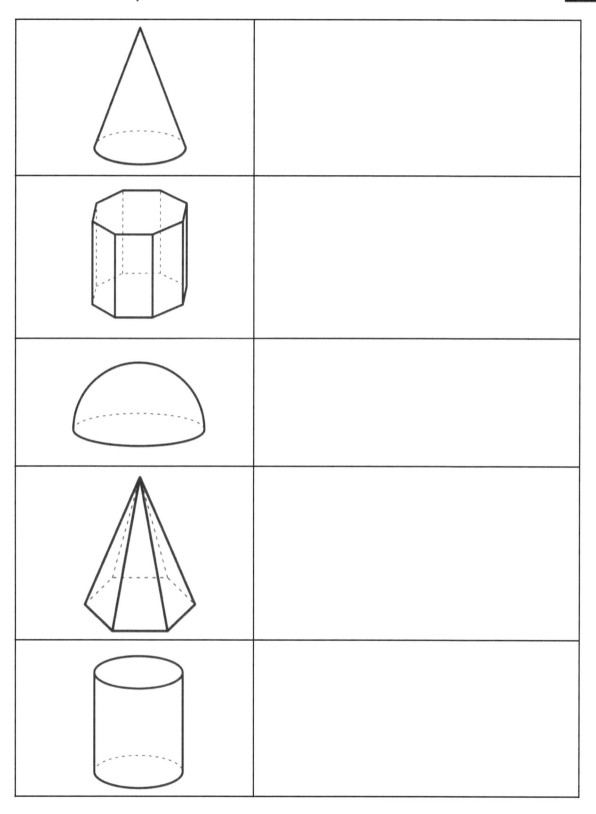

Score:

A) Here is a net of a 3-D shape.

When the net is folded, what 3-D shape will

it make?

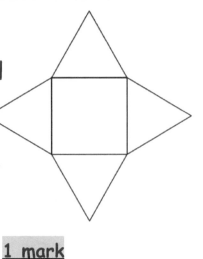

Put a ring around the correct answer below.

| | | |
|---|---|---|
| Cube | Prism | Cuboid |
| | Square-based pyramid | Triangular- based pyramid |

<u>1 mark</u>

B) Look at the cuboid below.

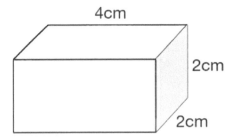

Draw two more faces to complete the net of the cuboid.

<u>1 mark</u>

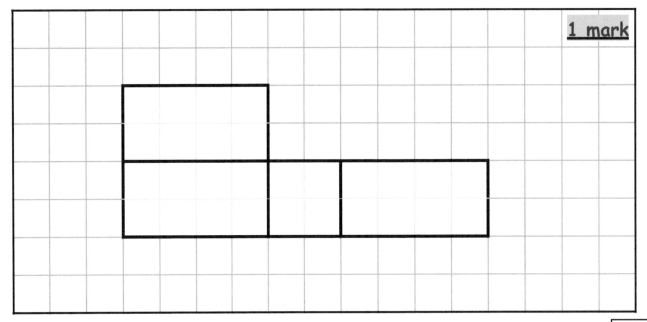

Score:

# Shape properties

## A) Complete the table.

| Name | Lines of symmetry | Number of equal-length sides | Number of equal angles |
|---|---|---|---|
| parallelogram | | 2 pairs | |
| Equilateral triangle | 3 | | |
| Regular octagon | | 8 | |
| Square | | | 4 |

## B) Classify these shapes.

8 marks

**Rectangle**   **Trapezium**   **Isosceles triangle**

**Parallelogram**   **Hexagon**   **Square**

**Right-angled triangle**   **Scalene triangle**

| | *Has at least one right angle* | *Has no right angles* |
|---|---|---|
| *Has more than 3 sides* | | |
| *Has less than 4 sides* | | |

Score:

A) The sum of the internal angles in a regular pentagon is 540°. Calculate the measurement of one internal angle in a regular pentagon. Show your working out.    <u>1 mark</u>

_____

_____

_____

B) Calculate the missing angles in the triangle    <u>2 marks</u>

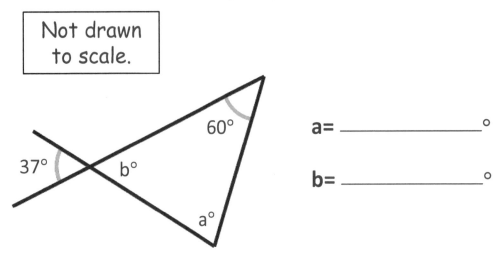

a= _____°

b= _____°

C) Calculate the internal angle labelled $x$ in this this irregular quadrilateral.    <u>1 mark</u>

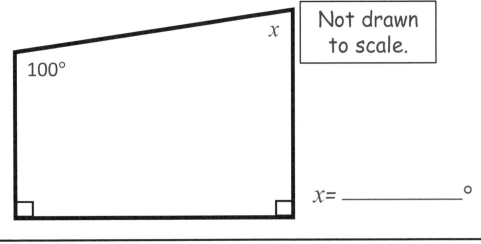

x= _____°

Score: [    ]

Label the parts of this circle.

1)

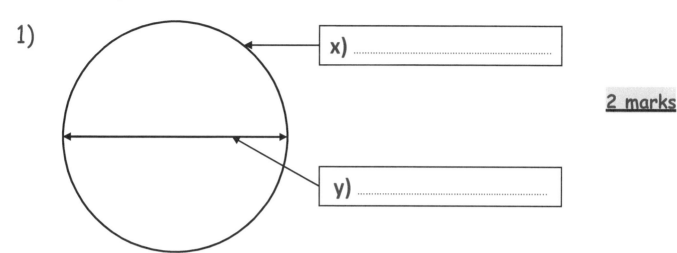

x) ......................................................

**2 marks**

y) ......................................................

2) On the circle above, illustrate and label the radius.  **1 mark**

*The formula for the diameter is :*

> **Diameter = 2 × Radius**
> **(D = 2 × R)**

3) The radius of a circle is 6cm. Calculate its diameter.

.................................................................................................. **1 mark**

4) The radius of a circle is 12.8cm. Calculate its diameter.

.................................................................................................. **1 mark**

5) The diameter of a circle is 13.4cm. Calculate its radius.

.................................................................................................. **1 mark**

6) The diameter of a circle is 50cm. Calculate its radius.

.................................................................................................. **1 mark**

Score:

A) Calculate the missing angles in the triangles.  **6 marks**

1)
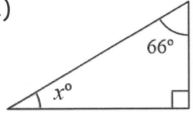
x= _____

2)
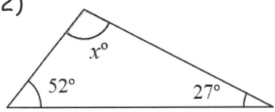
x= _____

3)
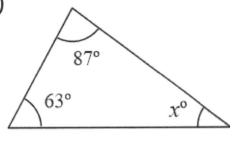
x= _____

4)
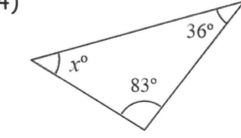
x= _____

5)
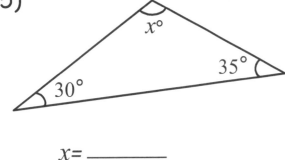
x= _____

6)
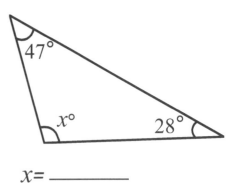
x= _____

B) Write the number of the triangles which has a missing acute/obtuse angle (x) in the question above. One has been done for you.  **5 marks**

| Acute angle | Obtuse angle |
|---|---|
| ① | |

Score: [     ]

The sum of the interior angles of a triangle is **180°**.

Split the polygons into triangles to work out the sum of their interior angles. Your lines should not overlap.    <u>15 marks</u>

1)
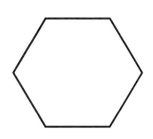

number of sides = ☐

number of triangles = ☐

☐ X 180 = ☐

The sum of the interior angles of a hexagon is ☐

2)

number of sides = ☐

number of triangles = ☐

☐ X 180 = ☐

The sum of the interior angles of a heptagon is ☐

3)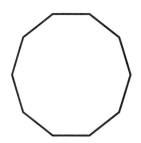

number of sides = ☐

number of triangles = ☐

☐ X 180 = ☐

The sum of the interior angles of a decagon is ☐

Score: ☐

A) What is the measurement of the angle labelled $x$ ?   <u>**1 mark**</u>

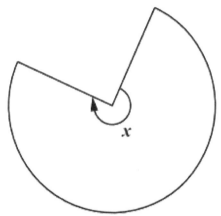

$x=$ _____ °

B) What is the measurement of the angle labelled $x$ ?   <u>**1 mark**</u>

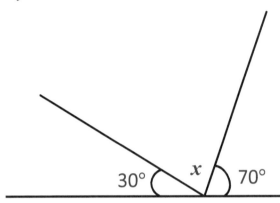

$x=$ _____ °

C) What is the measurement of the angle labelled $x$ ?   <u>**1 mark**</u>

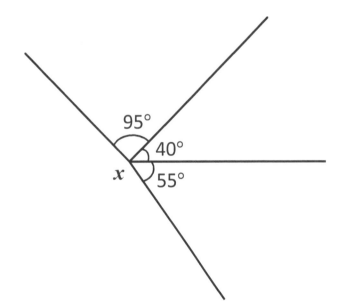

$x=$ _____ °

Score: ☐

Write the coordinates of the points A to F.     <u>12 marks</u>

1)

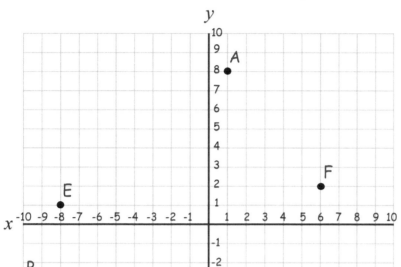

A ( —— , —— )

B ( —— , —— )

C ( —— , —— )

D ( —— , —— )

E ( —— , —— )

F ( —— , —— )

2)

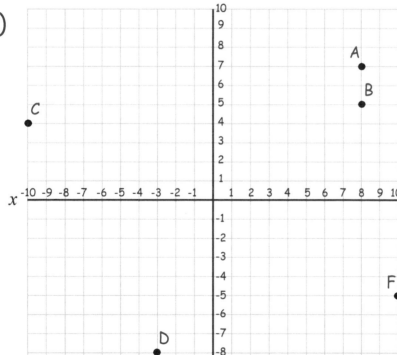

A ( —— , —— )

B ( —— , —— )

C ( —— , —— )

D ( —— , —— )

E ( —— , —— )

F ( —— , —— )

Score: [    ]

Plot the coordinates of the points A to D.

1)

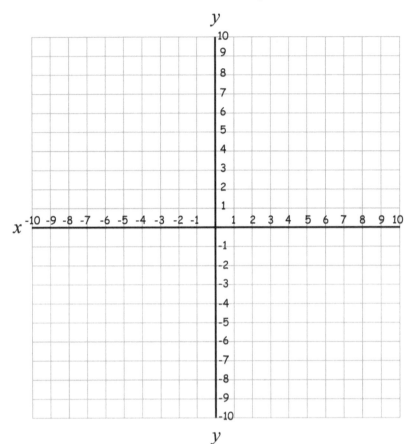

A  (-10, 5)

B  (-4, -6)

C  (5, -9)

D  (8, -1)

2)

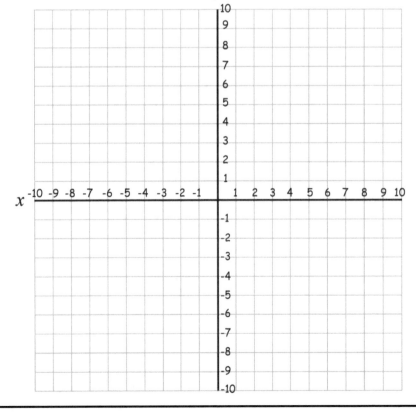

A  (5, -7)

B  (4, 8)

C  (-4, -3)

D  (-5, -6)

Score:

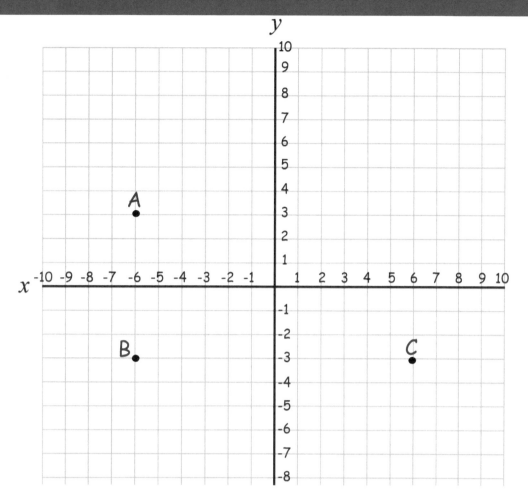

A) Write the coordinates of the   points A, B and C.   <u>3 marks</u>

A (———— , ————)     B (———— , ————)     C (———— , ————)

B) Draw lines to join the points A to C to form a   <u>1 mark</u>
triangle.

C) Write the coordinates of 4 different points in each
column of the table.   <u>12 marks</u>

| Inside the triangle | Outside the triangle | On the perimeter of the triangle |
|---|---|---|
| | | (2 , -3) |
| | | |

Score: [ ]

A) Label the coordinates of all of the vertices of each

shape.                                                        **14 marks**

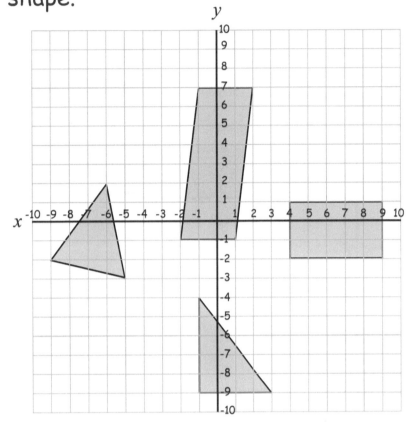

| Shape | Coordinates |
|---|---|
| △ | (— , —) (— , —) (— , —) |
| ▭ | (— , —) (— , —) (— , —) (— , —) |
| ▱ | (— , —) (— , —) (— , —) (— , —) |
| ◣ | (— , —) (— , —) (— , —) |

B) Complete the coordinates for these shapes.          **3 marks**

(2 , 8)        (4 , —)

(— , 5)        (4 , 5)

(-7 , -4)

(-10 , -10)   (— , -10)

Score: [    ]

A) Reflect the triangle in the *y*-axis.

1 mark

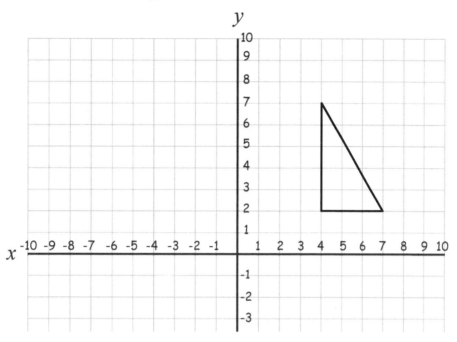

B) Reflect the shape in the *x*-axis.

1 mark

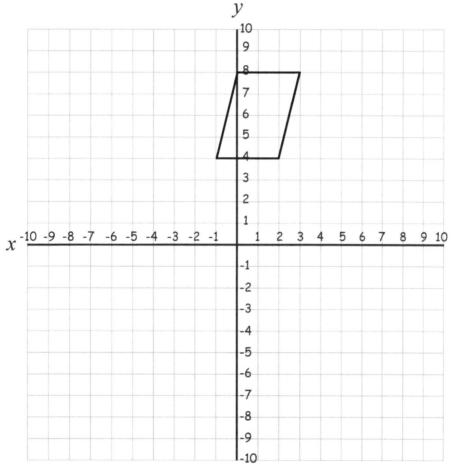

Score:

A) Translate this shape 7 places to the right.     1 mark

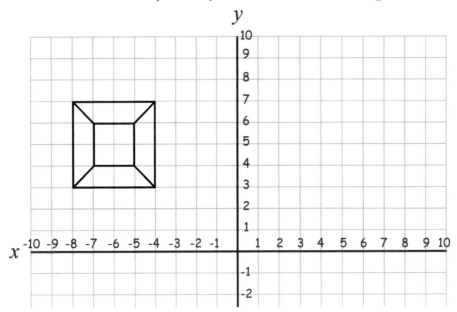

B) Use these coordinates to draw a shape:     4 marks
(1, -3) (4, 1) (1, 5) (-2, 1)

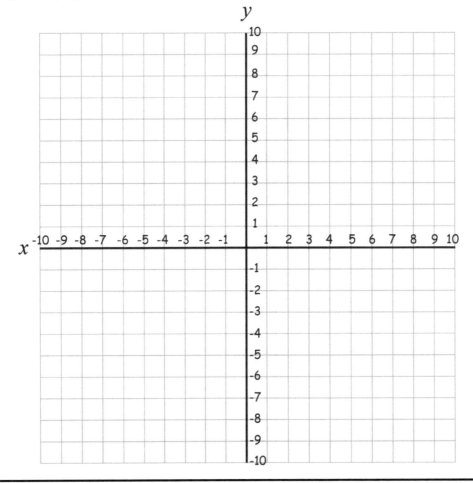

Score:

A) This shape is to be reflected in the $x$ axis, then translated 3 places left. Draw the new shape.

1 mark

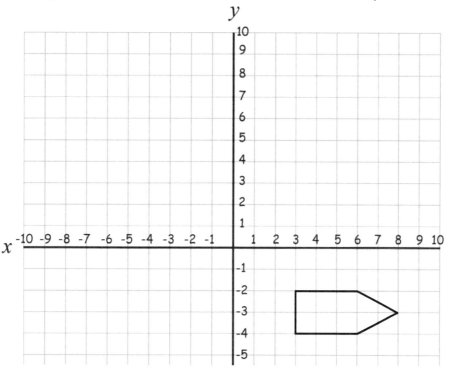

B) Translate the triangle 5 right and 9 down.

1 mark

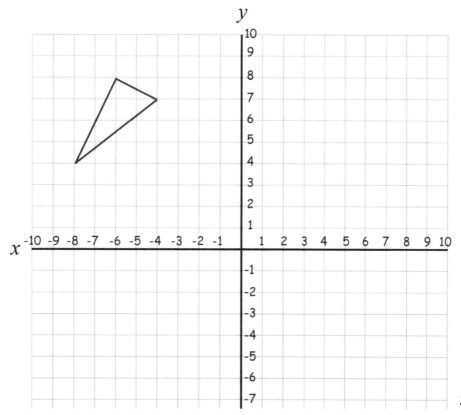

Score:

A) A shape is shown on the coordinate grid.

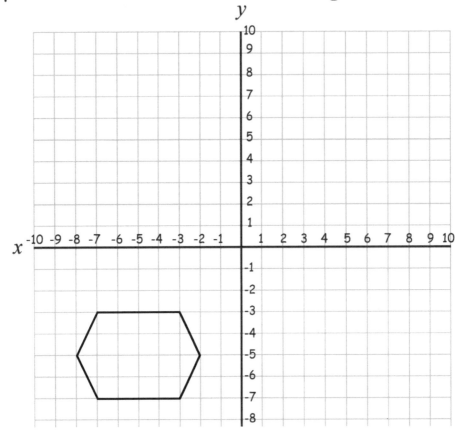

1) Reflect the shape in the $x$ axis.                          <u>1 mark</u>

2) Translate the new shape 10 right and 10 down.              <u>1 mark</u>

3) Reflect the new shape in the $x$ axis.                      <u>1 mark</u>

B) This shape is to be translated 8 places right.

Write down the new coordinates of its vertices.              <u>4 marks</u>

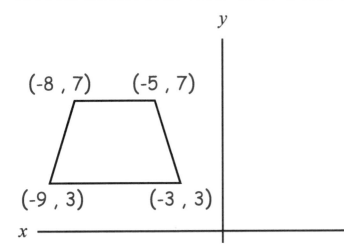

(——, ——)

(——, ——)

(——, ——)

(——, ——)

Score: [    ]

A) Draw the reflection of the shaded shape in the mirror line. Use a ruler.

1 mark

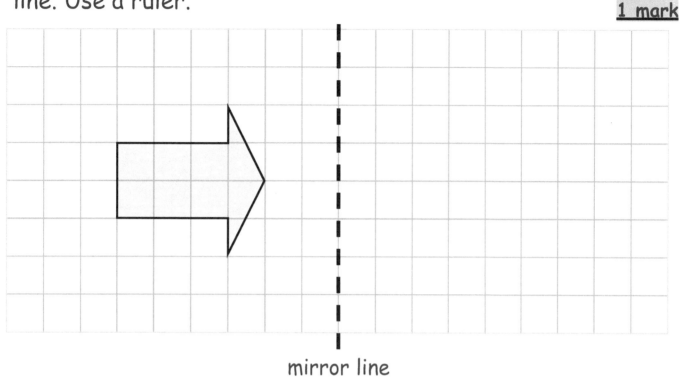

mirror line

B) The diamond shape is reflected in the mirror line. Draw the missing triangle and dots on the reflected diamond shape.

3 marks

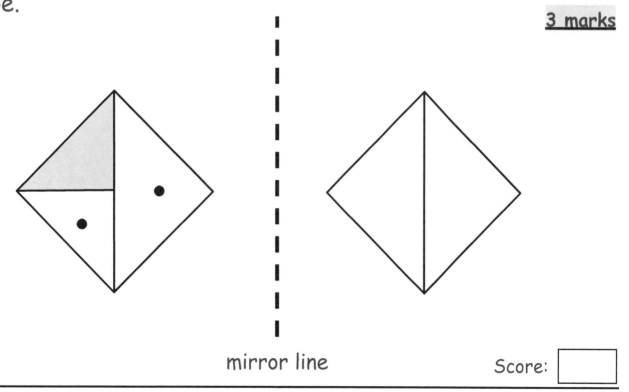

mirror line

Score:

A) Draw the reflection of the shaded shape in the mirror line. Use a ruler.

1 mark

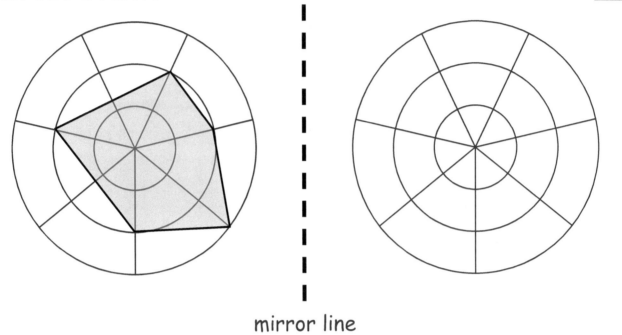

mirror line

B) The shape is translated so that point A moves to point B. Draw the shape in its new position.

1 mark

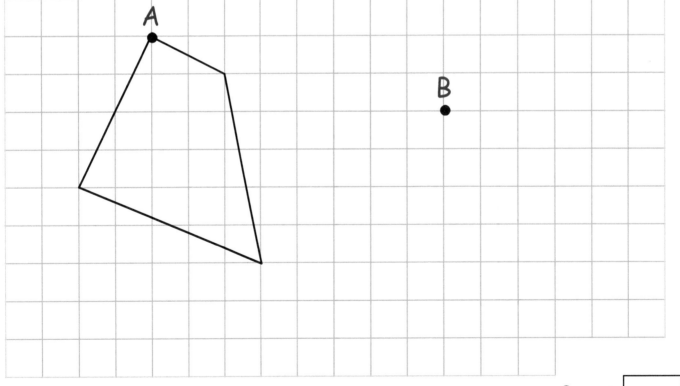

Score:

A) The pie chart shows the colours of toys in a supermarket.

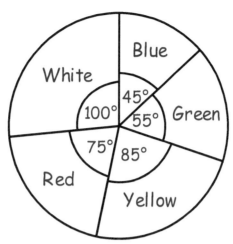

1) What is the most common colour of toys in the supermarket?                        **1 mark**

_____

2) What is the least common colour of toys?                        **1 mark**

_____

B) A group of football fans were asked who they supported. The pie chart and table show information about who they support.
Use the pie chart to complete the table.                        **6 marks**

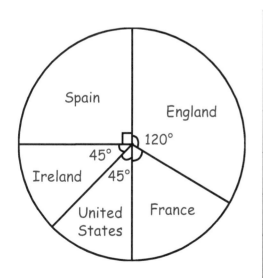

| Team | Angle of section | Number of fans |
|---|---|---|
| England | 120° | ...................... |
| France | ...................... | ...................... |
| United States | 45° | 6 |
| Ireland | 45° | ...................... |
| Spain | ...................... | ...................... |

Score: [ ]

A shop sells books, DVDs and video games.
This pie chart shows the sales of each in one week.

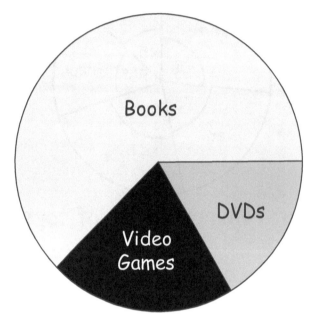

1) Estimate the **fraction** of the total sales that were    <u>2 marks</u>

books.

_____

_____

_____

_____

In this week, 140 video games were sold.

2) Estimate how many books were sold.    <u>2 marks</u>

_____

_____

_____

_____

_____    Score: [    ]

# Pie Charts

Some children were asked to name their favourite sports. 24 children surveyed altogether.
This chart shows their answers.

| Type of sport | Number of children |
|---|---|
| Swimming | 6 |
| Netball | 3 |
| Football | 12 |
| Gymnastics | 3 |

1) Use the frame below to create a pie chart to show this information. Use coloured pencil crayons and create a key to show what each section represents.

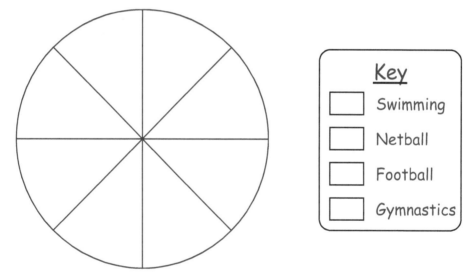

2) What percentage of children surveyed gave the answer football as their favourite sport?

3) What is the percentage difference between the number of children who answered swimming and gymnastics as their favourite sport?

Score:

Johnny and Olivia looked for foxes, squirrels, birds and worms in the woods.

They each made a pie chart of what they found.

*Johnny's pie chart*

*Olivia's pie chart*

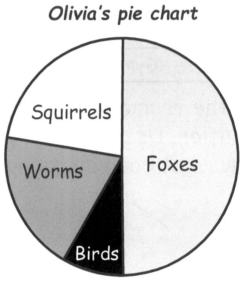

Total 120

Total 46

1) Estimate the number of squirrels that Johnny found.
<u>2 marks</u>

_____

_____

2) Who found more foxes? Circle Johnny or Olivia.

*Johnny*   *Olivia*   <u>1 mark</u>

3) Explain how you know.
<u>2 marks</u>

_____

_____

_____

_____   Score: [　　]

This line graph shows how many books are sold in a shop over six months.

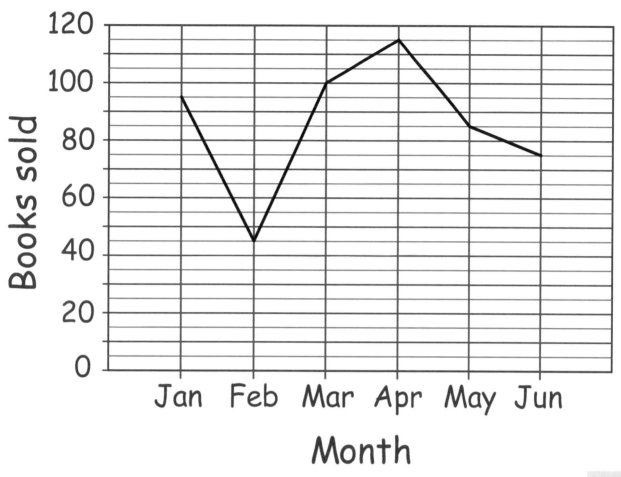

1) On which month did the shop sell the most books?          1 mark

_____

_____

2) On which month did the shop sell the least books?          1 mark

_____

_____

3) How many books were sold on May?          1 mark

_____

_____

Score: [     ]

This graph shows the temperature in °C from Monday to Sunday on a cold week.

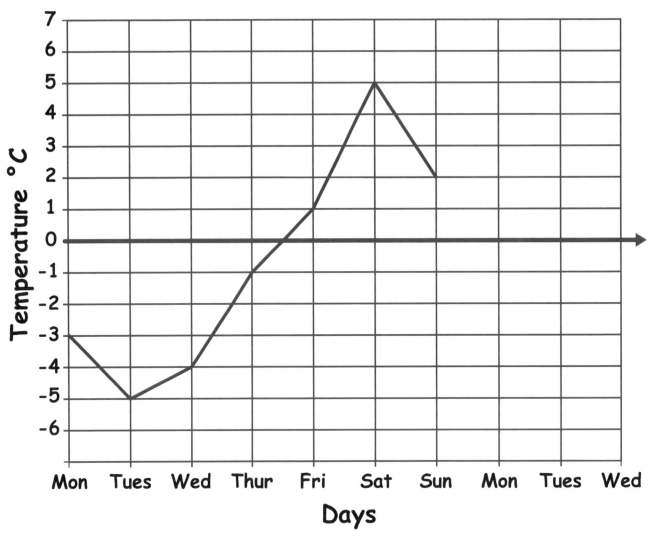

1) How many degrees **warmer** was on Sunday than Tuesday?

1 mark

_____

On Tuesday of the second week, the temperature was 6 degrees lower than Saturday.

2) What was the temperature on Tuesday of the second week?

1 mark

_____ Score: [    ]

The table below shows the population of London from 2002 to 2022.

| Year | Population |
|------|------------|
| 2002 | 7.3 Millions |
| 2007 | 7.6 Millions |
| 2012 | 8.3 Millions |
| 2017 | 8.9 Millions |
| 2022 | 9.5 Millions |

1) Plot the information as a line graph on the grid below.

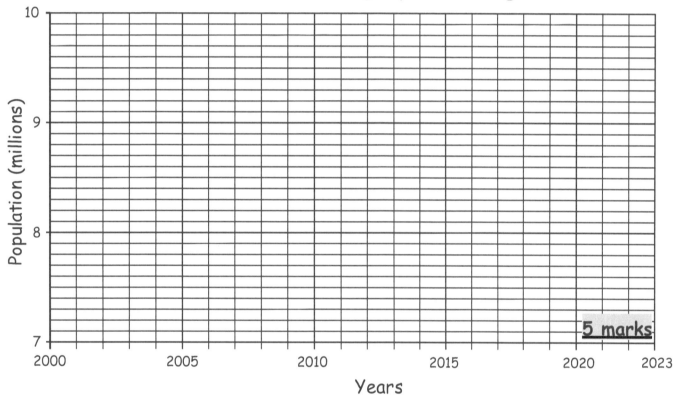

5 marks

2) Using the information in the graph, **estimate** London's approximate population in 2015.

1 mark

_____

3) Using the information in the graph, **predict** London's approximate population in 2023.

1 mark

_____

Score: ___

The table shows the number of customers each lunchtime at a chicken restaurant.

| Day | Customers |
|---|---|
| Monday | 37 |
| Tuesday | 42 |
| Wednesday | 2 |
| Thursday | 28 |
| Friday | 40 |
| Saturday | 49 |

1) Draw a line graph for the data.                     <u>6 marks</u>

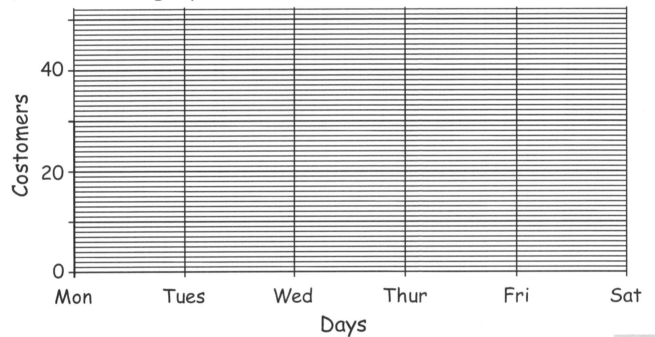

2) On which day did the restaurant have the most          <u>1 mark</u>
customers. _____

3) Work out how many customers visited the             <u>1 mark</u>
restaurant in total. _____

4) Give a possible reason why there were only 2 visitors <u>1 mark</u>
to the restaurant on Wednesday.

_____          Score: [    ]

# The Mean

A) Lily received a score of 97, 90, 95 and 94 on her first four maths exams. Find her average score.

| Mean = total ÷ number of items |
| --- |

1 mark

B) The school listed the number of students from Year 1 to Year 6:  40, 30, 36, 45, 32 and 27 . Find the mean number of students in each year.

1 mark

C) The table shows the temperature in different cities.

| City | Temperature (°C) |
| --- | --- |
| London | 18° |
| Aberdeen | 22° |
| Newcastle | 17° |
| Glasgow | 15° |
| Liverpool | 23° |
| Cardiff | 24° |
| Manchester | 21 ° |

Find her average temperature of the cities.

1 mark

Score:

# The Mean

**A)** Here are some cards with numbers on them.

| 1 | 2 | 3 | 5 | 7 | 12 | 20 |

**1)** Choose three numbers which have a mean of 5.    <u>1 mark</u>

_____

**2)** Choose four numbers which have a mean of 5.    <u>1 mark</u>

_____

**3)** Choose five numbers which have a mean of 5.    <u>1 mark</u>

_____

**B)** A, B and C stand for three different numbers.

### The mean of A and B is 30

### The mean of B and C is 45

### A + B + C = 120

Calculate the values of A, B and C.    <u>3 marks</u>

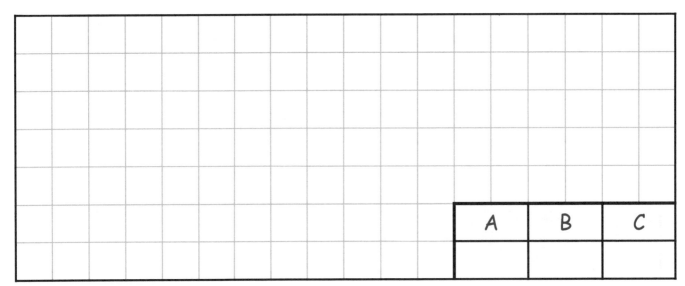

| | A | B | C |
|---|---|---|---|
| | | | |

Score: [    ]

# Answers

## Page 5:

**A)**

1. two million two hundred eighty-four thousand one hundred eighty-six

2. two million two hundred twenty-two thousand four hundred eighty-five

3. one million fifty-two thousand seven hundred twenty

4. one million six hundred ninety-two thousand seven hundred thirty-three

**B)**

1. 7,445,821    2. 2,307,627

3. 8,168,963

## Page 6:

**A)**

1. seven million one hundred thirty-four thousand one hundred seventy-six

2. six million one hundred fifty-four thousand six hundred twenty

3. five million three hundred ninety-one thousand one hundred five

4. seven million two hundred fifty-two thousand six

**B)**

1. 2,392,716    2. 4,343,961

3. 9,244,909

## Page 7:

1. 8,653,802    2. 6,144,545

3. 4,814,501    4. 2,339,038

5. 3,332,422    6. 9,022,221

7. 1,222,719    8. 3,203,232

## Page 8:

1. 3,000,000 + 900,000 + 90,000 + 4,000 + 300 + 10 + 3

2. 2,000,000 + 700,000 + 90,000 + 2,000 + 700 + 10 + 3

3. 1,000,000 + 800,000 + 50,000 + 1,000 + 100 + 40

4. 8,000,000 + 900,000 + 30,000 + 5,000 + 600 + 10 + 6

5. 8,000,000 + 700,000 + 50,000 + 2,000 + 400 + 80 + 4

6. 1,000,000 + 200,000 + 70,000 + 3,000 + 400 + 40 + 4

7. 6,000,000 + 100,000 + 70,000 + 6,000 + 400 + 80 + 5

8. 9,000,000 + 400,000 + 20,000 + 40 + 7

## Page 9:

1.
| 88,988 | 89,463 |
|--------|--------|
| 89,463 | 88,988 |
| 20,476 | 52,427 |
| 52,427 | 20,476 |

2.
| 53,948 | 99,610 |
|--------|--------|
| 49,184 | 76,689 |
| 99,610 | 53,948 |
| 76,689 | 49,184 |

3.  26,491    73,152
    73,152    60,016
    40,066    40,066
    60,016    26,491

4.  41,734    80,484
    80,484    54,449
    21,867    41,734
    54,449    21,867

5.  60,457    81,407
    77,355    77,355
    57,456    60,457
    81,407    57,456

6.  25,087    78,829
    63,162    63,162
    54,125    54,125
    78,829    25,087

7.  78,602    78,817
    50,275    78,602
    54,075    54,075
    78,817    50,275

8.  67,757    86,617
    86,617    73,236
    73,236    67,757
    43,362    43,362

*Page 10:*

1. <    2. <    3. <    4. >    5. <

6. >    7. >    8. >    9. <    10. <

11. >    12. <    13. >    14. >    15. <

16. >

*Page 11:*

1. 8 ten thousands

2. 4 ten thousands

3. 5 hundreds

4. 6 hundred thousands

5. 7 tens

6. 2 tens

7. 6 ten thousands

8. 6 tens

9. 4 millions

10. 9 ones

*Page 12:*

1. 3 millions + 8 hundred thousands + 9 ten thousands + 9 thousands + 1 hundred + 7 tens + 1 one

2. 5 millions + 6 hundred thousands + 6 ten thousands + 7 hundreds

3. 8 millions + 3 hundred thousands + 6 ten thousands + 6 thousands + 8 hundreds + 9 tens + 7 ones

4. 5 millions + 8 hundred thousands + 6 ten thousands + 8 thousands + 2 hundreds + 4 tens

5. 2 millions + 9 hundred thousands + 9 ten thousands + 8 thousands + 6 hundreds + 6 tens + 6 ones

6. 8 millions + 1 hundred thousand + 8 ten thousands + 3 thousands + 3 hundreds + 7 tens + 8 ones

## Page 13:
1. 854,210
2. 73,900
3. 90,000
4. 58,000
5. 813,150
6. 7,408,000
7. 681,200
8. 238,000
9. 839,000
10. 27,000
11. 30,000
12. 5,315,360
13. 7,960,000
14. 400,000
15. 350,000
16. 93,130
17. 1,930,000
18. 620,000
19. 12,780
20. 630,000

## Page 14:
1. 30,000
2. 2,165,000
3. 1,000,000
4. 1,855,730
5. 763,400
6. 9,570,000
7. 8,881,100
8. 695,700
9. 8,150,000
10. 20,000
11. 49,500
12. 50,000
13. 719,800
14. 38,050
15. 2,974,700
16. 53,200
17. 9,670,000
18. 361,620
19. 900,000
20. 400,000

## Page 15:
1. 26
2. 1
3. -6
4. 19
5. 3
6. 4
7. 7
8. 13
9. 10
10. -6
11. 21
12. 2
13. 10
14. -4
15. -11
16. -3
17. -6
18. 8
19. 23
20. -1

## Page 16:
1. 2
2. 13
3. 22
4. -14
5. -13
6. 2
7. -7
8. 7
9. -12
10. 4
11. -3
12. 13
13. 23
14. 6
15. 11
16. -11
17. 0
18. 8
19. 4
20. 5

## Page 17:
1. -$2.03
2. -$5.22
3. -$9.11
4. -$8.42
5. -$0.50
6. -$2.50
7. -$5.06
8. -$1.69
9. -$2.16
10. -$1.00

## Page 18:
A)
1. -5°C
2. -15°C
3. -10°C

B) 1°C

C) -13°C

D) 5°C

E) -23°C

## Page 19:
1. 406
2. 154
3. 844
4. 130
5. 825
6. 158
7. 321
8. 46
9. 407
10. 91
11. 54
12. 62
13. 89
14. 241
15. 425
16. 161
17. 187
18. 114
19. 564
20. 104

## Page 20:
1. 7,449
2. 14,390
3. 79,414
4. 58,371
5. 47,449
6. 76,729
7. 11,192
8. 16,382
9. 70,279
10. 10,479
11. 16,778
12. 7,741
13. 10,579
14. 85,787
15. 13,063
16. 70,243
17. 46,242
18. 55,260
19. 68,571
20. 78,421

## Page 21:
1. 134,609
2. 88,802
3. 78,395
4. 127,178
5. 177,981
6. 152,931
7. 113,331
8. 129,467
9. 112,684
10. 143,146
11. 136,668
12. 130,989
13. 129,035
14. 112,981
15. 58,301

## Page 22:
1. 107,314
2. 155,346
3. 167,917
4. 146,944
5. 113,382
6. 218,815
7. 219,195
8. 196,549
9. 155,906
10. 263,684
11. 131,105
12. 103,233

## Page 23:
1. 19
2. 39
3. 39
4. 13
5. 53
6. 10
7. 37
8. 5
9. 12
10. 1
11. 39
12. 65
13. 15
14. 53
15. 79
16. 10
17. 1
18. 44
19. 6
20. 37

## Page 24:
1. 593
2. 211
3. 6,166
4. 3,895
5. 455
6. 338
7. 5,219
8. 9,730
9. 3,289
10. 2,866
11. 8,046
12. 2,738
13. 550
14. 5,870
15. 3,379
16. 261
17. 219
18. 623
19. 3,086
20. 203

## Page 25:
1. 40,569
2. 22,667
3. 54,758
4. 2,798
5. 70,855
6. 65,628
7. 8,597
8. 31,789
9. 30,170
10. 39,204
11. 8,118
12. 42,648
13. 63,930
14. 28,614
15. 9,897

## Page 26:
1. 46,760
2. 73,125
3. 30,640
4. 13,712
5. 70,513
6. 88,032
7. 7,639
8. 32,594

9. 71,025     10. 54,693

11. 16,579     12. 93,672

13. 7,683     14. 38,104

15. 73,771

**Page 27:**

1. 8,000     2. 52

3. 0.07     4. 720

5. 0.43     6. 0.93

7. 0.56     8. 360

9. 73,200     10. 6,400

11. 5.2     12. 0.81

13. 32,000     14. 58,500

15. 0.66     16. 0.08

17. 11,900     18. 38.9

19. 168,000     20. 4,090

**Page 28:**

1. 13,560     2. 7,619,000

3. 58.52     4. 94

5. 86.24     6. 60,100

7. 0.65     8. 0.25

9. 92,530     10. 12,420

11. 8.84     12. 989.9

13. 527.2     14. 434,900

15. 743,000     16. 8,323,000

17. 8.43     18. 71.92

19. 750,000     20. 5,311,000

**Page 29:**

1. 12,627     2. 18,738

3. 16,737     4. 30,468

5. 5,506     6. 19,824

7. 29,655     8. 7,833

9. 11,456     10. 24,567

11. 15,888     12. 15,388

**Page 30:**

1. 79,528     2. 13,533

3. 41,345     4. 73,296

5. 35,945     6. 51,294

7. 28,768     8. 10,512

9. 23,466     10. 50,078

11. 32,208     12. 66,447

**Page 31:**

1. 20,808     2. 57,392

3. 36,545     4. 2,254

5. 65,088     6. 29,736

7. 51,201     8. 5,255

9. 4,738     10. 22,396

11. 49,861     12. 26,131

**Page 32:**

1. 69,408     2. 68,000

3. 3,627     4. 30,360

5. 33,240     6. 18,618

7. 16,873     8. 20,616

9. 56,145     10. 52,455

11. 81,005     12. 28,800

## Page 33:
| | |
|---|---|
| 1. 8,066 | 2. 15,402 |
| 3. 12,330 | 4. 12,610 |
| 5. 19,953 | 6. 42,559 |
| 7. 24,240 | 8. 32,852 |
| 9. 51,336 | 10. 3,264 |
| 11. 88,608 | 12. 69,355 |

## Page 34:
| | |
|---|---|
| 1. 35,259 | 2. 40,740 |
| 3. 53,417 | 4. 10,880 |
| 5. 23,870 | 6. 2,394 |
| 7. 68,632 | 8. 12,516 |
| 9. 53,040 | 10. 13,068 |
| 11. 8,720 | 12. 15,675 |

## Page 35:
| | |
|---|---|
| 1. 430,284 | 2. 140,000 |
| 3. 224,672 | 4. 524,718 |
| 5. 322,899 | 6. 136,059 |
| 7. 224,848 | 8. 303,892 |
| 9. 811,680 | 10. 123,168 |
| 11. 645,978 | 12. 138,640 |

## Page 36:
| | |
|---|---|
| 1. 441,882 | 2. 382,590 |
| 3. 648,088 | 4. 66,645 |
| 5. 116,493 | 6. 30,632 |
| 7. 573,678 | 8. 103,892 |
| 9. 107,203 | 10. 169,580 |
| 11. 741,320 | 12. 47,840 |

## Page 37:
| | |
|---|---|
| 1. 349,600 | 2. 239,316 |
| 3. 195,702 | 4. 365,050 |
| 5. 382,038 | 6. 226,973 |
| 7. 120,965 | 8. 720,720 |
| 9. 342,294 | 10. 213,768 |
| 11. 503,090 | 12. 458,131 |

## Page 38:
| | |
|---|---|
| 1. 375,785 | 2. 163,550 |
| 3. 564,224 | 4. 367,860 |
| 5. 58,160 | 6. 136,640 |
| 7. 834,200 | 8. 178,030 |
| 9. 85,120 | 10. 394,968 |
| 11. 263,432 | 12. 728,676 |

## Page 39:
| | | |
|---|---|---|
| 1. 1,960 | 2. 1,142 | 3. 741 |
| 4. 915 | 5. 788 | 6. 2,158 |
| 7. 424 | 8. 410 | 9. 1,151 |
| 10. 1,600 | 11. 1,314 | 12. 1,369 |

## Page 40:
| | | |
|---|---|---|
| 1. 986 | 2. 1,061 | 3. 2,316 |
| 4. 929 | 5. 152 | 6. 1,101 |
| 7. 3,277 | 8. 990 | 9. 314 |
| 10. 450 | 11. 615 | 12. 507 |

## Page 41:
| | | |
|---|---|---|
| 1. 922 | 2. 1,365 | 3. 1,104 |
| 4. 1,381 | 5. 704 | 6. 753 |
| 7. 4,903 | 8. 932 | 9. 771 |
| 10. 608 | 11. 625 | 12. 1,242 |

## Page 42:
1. 13   2. 7   3. 21   4. 7
5. 5   6. 4   7. 28   8. 6
9. 2   10. 8   11. 9   12. 16

## Page 43:
1. 12   2. 32   3. 2   4. 24
5. 13   6. 30   7. 5   8. 16
9. 12   10. 10   11. 8   12. 8

## Page 44:
1. 1   2. 5   3. 10   4. 21
5. 17   6. 5   7. 10   8. 4
9. 22   10. 7   11. 15   12. 11

## Page 45:
1. 135   2. 168   3. 73
4. 120   5. 121   6. 14
7. 297   8. 27   9. 84
10. 178   11. 84   12. 151

## Page 46:
1. 25   2. 220   3. 81
4. 168   5. 119   6. 297
7. 283   8. 31   9. 127
10. 463   11. 135   12. 64

## Page 47:
1. 7 R79   2. 42 R6
3. 21 R3   4. 17 R8
5. 15 R20   6. 4 R14
7. 10 R8   8. 53 R7
9. 39 R1   10. 14 R22
11. 23 R28   12. 2 R11

## Page 48:
1. 13 R8   2. 2 R52
3. 14 R21   4. 6 R7
5. 9 R21   6. 9 R52
7. 25 R22   8. 10 R79
9. 7 R45   10. 23 R1
11. 7 R34   12. 12 R12

## Page 49:
1. 11 R13   2. 34 R3
3. 1 R78   4. 13 R22
5. 3 R9   6. 19 R34
7. 14 R5   8. 11 R2
9. 14 R28   10. 2 R49
11. 7 R21   12. 15 R31

## Page 50:
1. 20 R17   2. 10 R35
3. 6 R68   4. 10 R38
5. 5 R56   6. 7 R2
7. 14 R2   8. 11 R16
9. 7 R19   10. 7 R62
11. 20 R17   12. 8 R40

## Page 51:
1. 128 R2   2. 15 R41
3. 63 R37   4. 5 R21
5. 127 R13   6. 251 R10
7. 159 R23   8. 69 R57
9. 263 R32   10. 225 R31
11. 49 R61   12. 9 R37

**_Page 52:_**

1. 502 R6      2. 471 R6

3. 9 R34       4. 34 R20

5. 375 R1      6. 8 R93

7. 211 R3      8. 171 R22

9. 46 R18      10. 215 R1

11. 4 R10      12. 1 R90

**_Page 53:_**

1. 160 R18     2. 104 R13

3. 104 R11     4. 108 R18

5. 135 R28     6. 125 R36

7. 102 R62     8. 65 R35

9. 42 R7       10. 73 R77

11. 96 R30     12. 239 R13

**_Page 54:_**

A)

1. 124 R39     2. 82 R29

3. 17 R13      4. 113 R49

5. 44 R61      6. 109 R10

B)

1. 16      2. 22

**_Page 55:_**

1. 16, 29   2. 13, 11   3. 3, 22

4. 17, 9    5. 3, 9     6. 10, 3

7. 27, 16   8. 20, 4    9. 16, 28

10. 19, 11

**_Page 56:_**

1. 15, 20   2. 4, 5     3. 15, 28

4. 14, 23   5. 4, 5     6. 13, 4

7. 21, 7    8. 8, 12    9. 15, 8

10. 23, 18

**_Page 57:_**

A)

1. 27       2. 101      3. 171

4. 99       5. 116      6. 120

7. 76       8. 126      9. 153

10. 123

B)

1. 7      2. 13    3. 34    4. 37

5. 11     6. 25    7. 45    8. 18

9. 29     10. 15

**_Page 58:_**

A)

1. 300      2. 1,260    3. 1,720

4. 2,640    5. 1,520    6. 420

7. 4,770    8. 6,160    9. 3,420

10. 1,600

B)

1. 5      2. 17    3. 16    4. 15

5. 3      6. 18    7. 23    8. 3

9. 24     10. 9

**_Page 59:_**

1. 65     2. 76     3. 73     4. 49
5. 79     6. 93     7. 38     8. 23

9. 35     10. 11

11. 44    12. 32    13. 52    14. 56

15. 68    16. 25    17. 10    18. 49

19. 39    20. 40

## Page 60:

1. 5  2. 18  3. 37  4. 59

5. 5  6. 3  7. 6  8. 7

9. 9  10. 26

11. 261  12. 153  13. 3

14. 120  15. 45  16. 160

17. 112  18. 80  19. 6

20. 232

## Page 61:

a.G  b.B  c.J  d.D  e.F  f.E

g.H  h.C  i.K  j.I  k.A

## Page 62:

1. 12 × 20 × 4 = 960

2. (14 + 19) ÷ 5 = 6.6

3. 10 + 5 + 5 = 20

4. 3 + 12 + 4 + 18 = 37

5. 3 + 17 + 16 = 36

6. 12 × 10 × 20 = 2,400

7. (19 + 17) ÷ 12 = 3

8. (14 × 8) + 9 = 121

9. 10 × (19 + 19) = 380

10. 9 + 19 + 16 = 44

11. (11 + 5) ÷ 16 = 1

12. 14 × (13 + 11) = 336

13. 18 + 6 − 14 + 7 = 17

14. 19 × 3 × 2 = 114

15. 7 + 12 − 20 + 11 = 10

16. 8 × (19 + 2) = 168

## Page 63:

A)

1. 1, 2, 4

2. 1, 2, 5, 10, 25, 50

3. 1, 3

4. 1, 2, 5, 10

5. 1, 97

6. 1, 2, 3, 4, 6, 9, 12, 18, 36

B)

1. 3  2. 6  3. 3

C)

1. 19 (Yes)  2. 3×3×7 (No)

3. 3×3 (No)  4. 67 (Yes)

## Page 64:

A)

1. 2, 4, 6, 8

2. 3, 6, 9, 12

3. 4, 8, 12, 16

4. 31, 62, 93, 124

5. 92, 184, 276, 368

6. 5, 10, 15, 20

7. 53, 106, 159, 212

8. 76, 152, 228, 304

9. 7, 14, 21, 28

10. 1, 2, 3, 4

B) 49  14  (21)  (42)  57

C) (6)  9  36  (2)  4

D) 72  (47)  (97)  65  (23)  95

E) 53 - 59 - 61 - 67 - 71 - 73 - 79 - 83 - 89 - 97

**Page 65:**

1. $3 + 9 + 18 + 2$

2. $(19 \times 4) - (2 + 19)$

3. $(12 + 2) \div 2$

4. $(9 + 2) \times (20 + 10)$

5. $(10 \times 14) - (20 + 20)$

6. $10 + 6 + 3 \times 5$

7. $13 \times (10 + 13)$

8. $16 + 3^2$

9. $11 \times (18 + 13)$

10. $8 \times (2 + 10)$

330
55
31
341
32
7
100
96
25
299

**Page 66:**

A) $3 + 4 \times 9$  and  $3 + (4 \times 9)$

B) $(5 \times 12) - 3$   ⟨$5 \times (12 - 3)$⟩   $5 \times 12 - 3$

C)

1. 2     2. 8     3. 7     4. 12

**Page 67:**

1. 22     2. 10     3. 84     4. 100

5. 17     6. 18     7. 5     8. 52

9. 21     10. 60

**Page 68:**

1. 1.4     2. 13     3. 1     4. 78

5. 4     6. 47     7. 23     8. 196

9. 23     10. 98

**Page 69:**

1. 90     2. 157     3. 102

4. 37     5. 104     6. 288

7. 102     8. 53     9. 42

10. 135

**Page 70:**

1. 338     2. 3     3. 62     4. 80

5. -1     6. 31     7. 100     8. 432

9. 30     10. -7

**Page 71:**

1. 14,620     2. 14,139

3. 63,414     4. 80,813

5. 73,444     6. 29,014

7. 30     8. 21

9. 19,490     10. 9

11. 3,740     12. 12,873

**Page 72:**

A)

1. 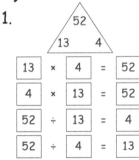     2.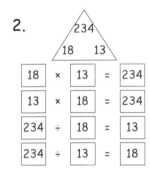

B)

1. 44     2. 80     3. 37

C) a.A     b.D     c.B     d.C

**Page 73:**

1. 11/12     2. 4/5     3. 3/4

4. 9/16     5. 1/5     6. 2/7

7. 1/6     8. 7/9     9. 5/6

10. 11/12     11. 3/4     12. 7/8

13. 1/3     14. 6/11     15. 4/5

## Page 74:

1. 1/2      2. 3/5      3. 1/6
4. 17/32    5. 4/7      6. 1/2
7. 2/3      8. 2/11     9. 1/3
10. 13/18   11. 2/5     12. 8/9
13. 5/8     14. 3/8     15. 17/20

## Page 75:

1. 1/2      2. 3/10     3. 1/2
4. 1/9      5. 1/3      6. 3/8
7. 4/5      8. 1/3      9. 1/2
10. 5/6     11. 7/9     12. 3/7
13. 13/24   14. 3/11    15. 5/32

## Page 76:

1. 21/100   2. 2/3      3. 2/3
4. 4/7      5. 3/5      6. 1/9
7. 13/20    8. 1/8      9. 1/6
10. 1/2     11. 3/5     12. 7/9
13. 2/5     14. 3/20    15. 1/4

## Page 77:

1. >    2. >    3. >    4. <    5. <
6. <    7. >    8. >    9. <    10. >
11. <   12. <

## Page 78:

1. >    2. <    3. >    4. <    5. >
6. >    7. >    8. <    9. >    10. >
11. <   12. >

## Page 79:

1.

2.

3.

4.

## Page 80:

1.

2.

3.

4.

## Page 81:
A)

1. 1 1/10    2. 15/16    3. 5/8
4. 1 1/4     5. 1 1/21   6. 1 4/21

B)

1. 1/21      2. 37/88    3. 2/5
4. 1/20      5. 23/48    6. 3/56

## Page 82:
A)

1. 3/1       2. 17/9     3. 6/1
4. 1/3       5. 13/2     6. 1/7

**B)**

1. 23/2      2. 118/9      3. 127/12

4. 57/8      5. 109/18     6. 101/7

**Page 83:**
**A)**

1. **6** 83/224        2. **5** 19/24

3. **3** 7/80          4. **9** 2/3

5. **10** 11/45        6. **2** 7/24

**B)**

1. **8** 43/55         2. **8** 71/90

3. **8** 14/15         4. **3** 23/30

5. **5** 3/20          6. **8** 11/28

**Page 84:**
**A)**

1. **7** 55/72         2. **17** 31/90

3. 15                  4. **16** 17/70

5. **13** 11/42        6. **7** 11/20

**B)**

1. **6** 8/15          2. 2/3

3. 9/70                4. 1/4

5. **2** 60/77         6. 20/63

**Page 85:**

1. 1/4        2. 1/10       3. 1/4

4. 5/32       5. 1/3        6. 1/10

7. 9/56       8. 3/16       9. 8/21

10. 6/35      11. 3/10      12. 5/56

13. 1/5       14. 2/7

**Page 86:**

1. 4/7        2. 3/14       3. 1/4

4. 1/4        5. 1/40       6. 2/9

7. 5/56       8. 1/12       9. 1/21

10. 1/4       11. 9/22      12. 3/16

13. 1/14      14. 1/21

**Page 87:**

1. 4          2. **2** 2/11     3. 3

4. **1** 2/3      5. **1** 5/7      6. **2** 2/3

7. **2** 2/3      8. 2          9. **2** 2/3

10. **1** 1/2     11. 3         12. **1** 1/2

13. 4         14. **5** 1/7

**Page 88:**

1. **3** 3/7      2. 2          3. **7** 7/8

4. **3** 3/5      5. 2          6. **3** 1/2

7. **2** 1/2      8. 2          9. 1

10. **4** 4/5     11. 2/3       12. **1** 7/11

13. **2** 2/3     14. 4

**Page 89:**

1. 1/6        2. 3/25       3. 5/21

4. 1/27       5. 1/12       6. 1/14

7. 2/21       8. 1/9        9. 1/14

10. 1/24      11. 3/25      12. 1/18

13. 1/16      14. 2/35

**Page 90:**

1. 1/12       2. 1/2        3. 1/2

4. 3/16       5. 1/4        6. 2/7

7. 1/6        8. 2/21       9. 7/16

10. 1/10    11. 1/6    12. 7/24

13. 1/3    14. 1/21

**Page 91:**

A)

1. 26.0          2. 627.0

3. 6,880.0       4. 96.0

5. 82.0          6. 530.00

7. 72.00         8. 960.0

B)

1. 38.89         2. 5.74

3. 6.9           4. 836.76

5. 8.48          6. 4.3

7. 6,474         8. 0.04

**Page 92:**

A)

1. 1,060.00      2. 46.0

3. 54.00         4. 430.0

5. 900.0         6. 338.0

7. 91.80         8. 45.00

B)

1. 0.068    2. 7.6    3. 0.922

4. 0.029    5. 0.812    6. 0.0692

7. 0.0938    8. 21.39

**Page 93:**

1. 0.36          2. 28.2

3. 44.1          4. 1,327.7

5. 67.08         6. 1.68

7. 71.20         8. 44.0

9. 15.2          10. 329.94

11. 446.4        12. 0.25

13. 3.2          14. 5.6

15. 4,303.6      16. 473.2

**Page 94:**

1. 18.6          2. 17.10

3. 1.2           4. 1.62

5. 33.6          6. 0.18

7. 4.0           8. 0.90

9. 584.5         10. 0.15

11. 3.28         12. 54.36

13. 3.2          14. 560.4

15. 328.18       16. 0.93

**Page 95:**

1. 2.08          2. 176.4

3. 5,997.6       4. 7.44

5. 6.93          6. 14.46

7. 185.74        8. 221.5

9. 336.0         10. 620.9

11. 52.80        12. 1,820.7

13. 4.45         14. 73.5

15. 1.26         16. 4.38

**Page 96:**

1. 12.00         2. 22.2

3. 3.30          4. 44.03

5. 1.40          6. 4.8

7. 49.28         8. 114.0

9. 261.8    10. 207.5

11. 81.54    12. 622.52

13. 88.2    14. 971.7

15. 417.6    16. 19.11

*Page 97:*

1. 32.8    2. 116

3. 285.67    4. 135.5

5. 101    6. 90.4

7. 147.2    8. 104.57

9. 124.63

*Page 98:*

1. 54.5    2. 58.71

3. 194.67    4. 86.5

5. 84.67    6. 243.67

7. 111.67    8. 118.2

9. 81.67

*Page 99:*

1. 0.50    2. 9.63    3. 6.5

4. 13.72    5. 1.14    6. 10.97

7. 0.29    8. 15.98    9. 1.05

*Page 100:*

1. 10.74    2. 13.58    3. 0.98

4. 0.30    5. 2.63    6. 0.87

7. 0.74    8. 13.96    9. 3.90

*Page 101:*

1. 0.93    2. 0.05    3. 8.2

4. 1    5. 99.3    6. 0.69

7. 3.73    8. 6.43    9. 8

10. 3.2    11. 2    12. 3.54

13. 1    14. 37    15. 0

16. 0.98    17. 1    18. 2

19. 0.7    20. 0.3

*Page 102:*

1. 0.8    2. 3.27    3. 10

4. 17    5. 71    6. 0

7. 0.25    8. 0.2    9. 0

10. 0.5    11. 0    12. 0.87

13. 1    14. 6    15. 5.7

16. 0    17. 18.4    18. 0.4

19. 0    20. 0.04

*Page 103:*

A)

1. 0.5    2. 0.53    3. 0.8

4. 0.05    5. 0.54    6. 0.46

7. 0.7    8. 0.42    9. 0.69

10. 0.9    11. 0.08    12. 0.15

B)

1. 3/10    2. 4/25    3. 1/2

4. 1/10    5. 2/5    6. 3/5

7. 9/100    8. 4/5

*Page 104:*

A)

1. 0.89    2. 0.67    3. 0.03

4. 0.5    5. 0.72    6. 0.8

7. 0.4    8. 0.5

**B)**

| | | |
|---|---|---|
| 1. 4/5 | 2. 2/7 | 3. 2/3 |
| 4. 1/2 | 5. 37/50 | 6. 11/25 |
| 7. 2/5 | 8. 1/8 | 9. 1/3 |
| 10. 4/9 | 11. 3/4 | 12. 1/6 |

## Page 105:
**A)**

| | | |
|---|---|---|
| 1. 33% | 2. 71% | 3. 69% |
| 4. 13% | 5. 43% | 6. 89% |
| 7. 62% | 8. 10% | 9. 61% |
| 10. 57% | 11. 99% | 12. 79% |

**B)**

| | | |
|---|---|---|
| 1. 0.49 | 2. 0.91 | 3. 0.4 |
| 4. 0.97 | 5. 0.18 | 6. 0.56 |
| 7. 0.51 | 8. 0.35 | |

## Page 106:
**A)**

| | | |
|---|---|---|
| 1. 93% | 2. 17% | 3. 10% |
| 4. 90% | 5. 33% | 6. 4% |
| 7. 28% | 8. 41% | |

**B)**

| | | |
|---|---|---|
| 1. 0.95 | 2. 0.48 | 3. 0.63 |
| 4. 0.31 | 5. 0.39 | 6. 0.76 |
| 7. 0.02 | 8. 0.09 | 9. 0.67 |
| 10. 0.93 | 11. 0.25 | 12. 0.78 |

## Page 107:
**A)** $2.1

**B)**

1. Peanut butter 375g     Sugar 210g

    3 Large egg     3 teaspoon vanilla

2. 4 cookies

## Page 108:
**A)**

| | | |
|---|---|---|
| 1. $30 | 2. $45 | 3. $45 |

**B)** $9

**C)** 150g

**D)** $1.25

## Page 109:

1. 2      2. 3

## Page 110:

1. 5      2. 2

## Page 111:

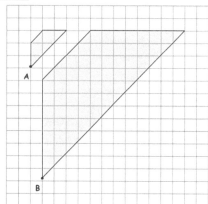

## Page 112:

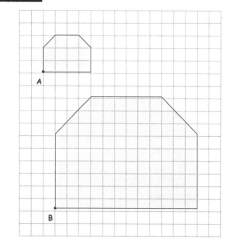

## Page 113:
**A)**

1. 11    2. 115    3. 21    4. 36

5. 162

**B)**

1. $45.75    2. $10.65

3. $70.70    4. $19.20

5. $16.00

*Page 114:*

**A)**

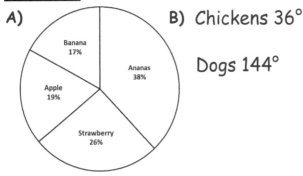

**B)** Chickens 36°

Dogs 144°

*Page 115:*

**A)** 30 seeds

**B)** 3 : 1

**C)** 72

*Page 116:*

**A)** 3/8 of 120 = 45, so Olivia and Harrison have both read 45 pages

**B)** 30 goats

**C)** 9 potatoes

*Page 117:*

1. 20    2. 11    3. 19    4. 10    5. 14

6. 18    7. 5    8. 19    9. 7    10. 8

*Page 118:*

1. 17    2. 2    3. 14    4. 7

5. 12    6. 18    7. 18    8. 20

9. 15    10. 4

*Page 119:*

**A)**

1. 15    2. -22    3. 31    4. 7

5. 17    6. 81

**B)**

1. 155    2. 29    3. 197    4. 26

*Page 120:*

1. 10    2. 72    3. 6

4. 156    5. 21    6. -12

7. 28    8. 48    9. 41

10. -22

*Page 121:*

**A)**

1.

| 6 | 11 | 16 | 21 | 26 | 31 | 36 | 41 | 46 |
|---|----|----|----|----|----|----|----|----|

2.

| 16 | 24 | 32 | 40 | 48 | 56 | 64 | 72 | 80 |
|----|----|----|----|----|----|----|----|----|

**B)**

1.

| Input | Output |
|-------|--------|
| 56 | 1,400 |
| 7 | 175 |
| 51 | 1,275 |
| 36 | 900 |

Multiply by 25

2.

| Input | Output |
|-------|--------|
| 702 | 18 |
| 663 | 17 |
| 1,833 | 47 |
| 1,248 | 32 |

Divide by 39

3.

| Input | Output |
|-------|--------|
| 9 | 378 |
| 48 | 2,016 |
| 52 | 2,184 |
| 44 | 1,848 |

Multiply by 42

4.

| Input | Output |
|-------|--------|
| 39 | 468 |
| 6 | 72 |
| 26 | 312 |
| 14 | 168 |

Multiply by 12

*Page 122:*

**A)**

| Input | 5 | 3 | 3.2 | - 5 | 5 | 28 | -6 | - 7 |
|---|---|---|---|---|---|---|---|---|
| Output | 12 | 10 | 10.2 | 2 | 12 | 35 | 1 | 0 |

**B)**   1. 10        2. 40        3. 2n - 4

*Page 123:*

**A)**   1. 28        2. 26

**B)**   Total interior angles = 360°
120 + 60 + 80 + b = 360
260 + b = 360
b = 360 – 260
b = 100°

*Page 124:*

**A)**   1.  - 12y - 11        2. - 10y + 32
         3. 24y - 3           4. - 3y - 5

**B)**

1.

(13+y=42)        42=y-13        y=13+42        y= 29

2.

y-12=37        (12+y=37)        y+12=37        y= 25

3.

22-y=14        14-y=22        (y-14=22)        y= 36

*Page 125:*

A) If a= 1 , b= 7        If a= 2 , b= 4
   If a= 3 , b= 1

B) a = 16 & b = 4 does not satisfy the equation.

C) x= 8  &  y= 3    ,    x= 12  &  y= 2
   x= 6  &  y= 4

*Page 126:*

A) ♡ = 8        ☺ = 4

B) 1. True        2. False        3. True
   4. False

**C)**

| Value of c | Value of d |
|---|---|
| 5 | 17 |
| 2 | 2 |
| 7 | 27 |
| 4 | 12 |

*Page 127:*

**A)**

1. 18,000        2. 60,000

3. 0.048        4. 19,000

5. 0.056        6. 68,000

7. 30,000        8. 0.045

**B)**

1. 728 wk        2. 0 min 27 sec

3. 0 hr 23 min        4. 126 dy

5. 0 hr 16 sec        6. 1,140 sec

7. 672 hr        8. 0 dy 20 hr

*Page 128:*

**A)**

1. 0.51        2. 0.71        3. 0.024

4. 0.052        5. 740        6. 450

7. 0.040        8. 720

**B)**

1. 1,500 min        2. 0 min 15 sec

3. 0 dy 11 hr        4. 1,320 sec

5. 360 hr        6. 1,092 wk

7. 3 wk 2 dy        8. 3,650 dy

*Page 129:*

**A)**

1. 1.609        2. 197.949

3. 785.360        4. 336.353

5. 523.037        6. 687.190

**B)**

1. 79.536  2. 267.811

3. 65.865  4. 41.010

5. 111.847  6. 128.624

**C)**

1. 336 hr  2. 0 dy 10 hr

3. 6,205 dy  4. 0 hr 15 min

5. 728 wk  6. 0 min 19 sec

**Page 130:**

**A)**

1. 1,196 wk  2. 2 wk 5 dy

3. 7,300 dy  4. 0 hr 21 sec

5. 0 min 26 sec  6. 1,380 min

**B)**

1. 83.686  2. 634.082

3. 114.263  4. 310.603

5. 326.697  6. 289.682

**C)**

1. 52.195  2. 305.093

3. 37.282  4. 259.733

5. 37.904  6. 172.120

**Page 131:**

1. A=165  2. A=112

3. A=27.72  4. A=27.71

5. A=62.35  6. A=72

**Page 132:**

1. A=125.14  2. A=52.39

3. A=50.04  4. A=65

5. A=120  6. A=60

**Page 133:**

1. A=36  2. A=48  3. A=88

4. A=80  5. A=42  6. A=32

**Page 134:**

1. A=120  2. A=42  3. A=80

4. A=210  5. A=176  6. A=110

**Page 135:**

1. P=60  A=150  2. P=49  A=105

3. P=34  A=72  4. P=54  A=168

**Page 136:**

1. P=74  A=340  2. P=44  A=90

3. P=31  A=40  4. P=35  A=48

**Page 137:**

1. 12  2. 10  3. 30  4. 10

5. 25  6. 24

**Page 138:**

1. 60  2. 48  3. 18  4. 50

5. 30  6. 24

**Page 139:**

1. 36  2. 18  3. 56  4. 52

5. 40  6. 10

**Page 140:**

1. 52  2. 12  3. 7  4. 94

5. 34  6. 11

**Page 141:**

1. V=336 cm$^3$

2. V=1,001 cm$^3$

3. V=576 cm$^3$

4. V=36 cm$^3$

## Page 142:

1. V=1,248 cm³

2. V=630 cm³

3. V=210 cm³

4. V=72 cm³

## Page 143:

1. V=60 cm³

2. V=1,456 cm³

3. V=36 cm³

4. V=16 cm³

## Page 144:

| Shape 1 | < > or = | Shape 2 |
|---|---|---|
|  7 cm, 5 cm, 5 cm | < | 10 cm, 6 cm, 7 cm |
| 6 cm, 9 cm, 8 cm | > | 2 cm, 2 cm, 4 cm |
| 4 cm, 8 cm, 4 cm | = | 4 cm, 16 cm, 2 cm |
| 13 cm, 17 cm, 13 cm | < | 22 cm, 33 cm, 21 cm |

## Page 145:

A)

B)

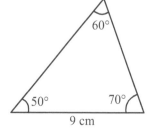

## Page 146:

A)

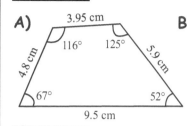

B) Measurements should be to the nearest millimetre.

## Page 147:

A)

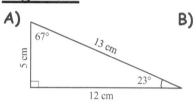

B)

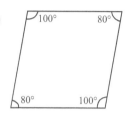

## Page 148:

A)

| Name | Number of Faces | Number of Edges | Number of Vertices | number of curved faces |
|---|---|---|---|---|
| Cuboid | 6 | 12 | 8 | 0 |
| Triangular Prism | 5 | 9 | 6 | 0 |
| Pentagonal Prism | 7 | 15 | 10 | 0 |
| Triangular Pyramid | 4 | 6 | 4 | 0 |
| Hexagonal Prism | 8 | 18 | 12 | 0 |

B)

| Properties | Name of shape |
|---|---|
| 5 vertices and 5 faces. | Square pyramid |
| 0 flat faces, 1 curved face, 0 edges, 0 vertices. | Sphere |
| 2 flat faces, 1 curved face, 2 edges, 0 vertices. | Cylinder |
| 1 flat face, 1 curved face, 1 edge, 1 vertex. | Cone |

C) rectangle      pyramid      (cube)

cylinder      square

## Page 149:

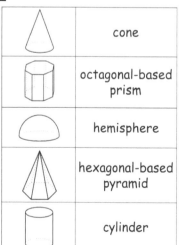

| | |
|---|---|
| | cone |
| | octagonal-based prism |
| | hemisphere |
| | hexagonal-based pyramid |
| | cylinder |

## Page 150:

A)

| Cube | Prism | Cuboid |
| --- | --- | --- |
| (Square-based pyramid) | | Triangular-based pyramid |

B)

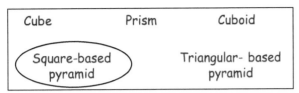

The square could have been here

Rectangle could have been here

## Page 151:

A)

| Name | Lines of symmetry | Number of equal-length sides | Number of equal angles |
| --- | --- | --- | --- |
| parallelogram | 0 | 2 pairs | 4 |
| Equilateral triangle | 3 | 3 | 3 |
| Regular octagon | 8 | 8 | 8 |
| Square | 4 | 4 | 4 |

B)

| | Has at least one right angle | Has no right angles |
| --- | --- | --- |
| Has more than 3 sides | Square Rectangle | Hexagon Trapezium Parallelogram |
| Has less than 4 sides | Right-angled triangle | Scalene triangle Isosceles triangle |

## Page 152:

A) 540 ÷ 5 = 108°

B) a= 83°     b= 37°

C) x= 80°

## Page 153:

1.

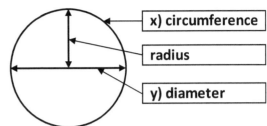

x) circumference

radius

y) diameter

2. Radius is illustrated and labelled appropriately

3. D= 2 × 6 = 12 cm

4. D= 2 × 12.8 = 25.6 cm

5. R= D ÷ 2 = 13.4 ÷ 2 = 6.7 cm

6. R= D ÷ 2 = 50 ÷ 2 = 25 cm

## Page 154:

A)  1. 24°    2. 101°    3. 30°
    4. 61°    5. 115°    6. 105°

B)

| Acute angle | Obtuse angle |
| --- | --- |
| ① ③ ④ | ② ⑤ ⑥ |

## Page 155:

1.

number of sides = 6
number of triangles = 4
3 X 180 = 540
The sum of the interior angles of a hexagon is 540°

2.

number of sides = 7
number of triangles = 5
5 X 180 = 900
The sum of the interior angles of a heptagon is 900°

3.

number of sides = 10
number of triangles = 8
8 X 180 = 1440
The sum of the interior angles of a decagon is 1440°

## Page 156:

A) $x$ = 270°

B) $x$ = 80°

C) $x$ = 170°

## Page 157:

1.  A $(1 , 8)$   B $(-10 , -3)$   C $(-5 , -8)$
    D $(5 , -9)$     E $(-8 , 1)$     F $(6 , 2)$

2.  A $(8 , 7)$     B $(8, 5)$       C $(-10 , 4)$
    D $(-3 , -8)$ E $(8 , -10)$ F $(10 , -5)$

## Page 158:

1.

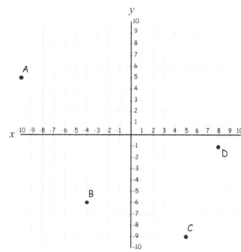

2.

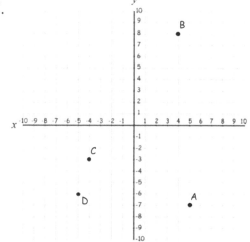

## Page 159:

A)   A $(-6 , 3)$ ;     B $(-6 , -3)$ ;
     C $(6 , -3)$

B)

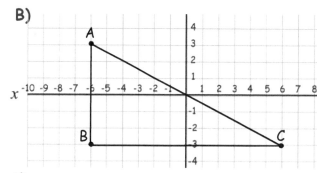

C)

| Inside the triangle | Outside the triangle | On the perimeter of the triangle |
|---|---|---|
| $(-5 , 1)$ $(-1 , -1)$ $(-3 , 1)$ $(-2 , -2)$ | $(2 , 2)$ $(7 , -4)$ $(-4 , -7)$ $(-3 , 4)$ | $(2 , -3)$ $(-4 , 2)$ $(-4 , -3)$ $(3 , -3)$ |

## Page 160:

A)

| Shape | Coordinates | |
|---|---|---|
| △ | $(-6 , 2)$   $(-5 , -3)$  $(-9 , -2)$ | |
| ▭ | $(4 , 1)$   $(9 , 1)$  $(4 , -2)$   $(9 , -2)$ | |
| ▱ | $(2 , 7)$   $(-1 , 7)$  $(1 , -1)$   $(-2 , -1)$ | |
| ◿ | $(-1 , -4)$   $(-1 , -9)$  $(3 , -9)$ | |

B)

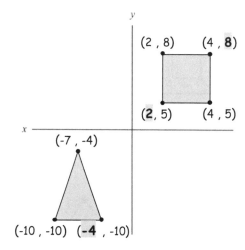

## Page 161:

A)

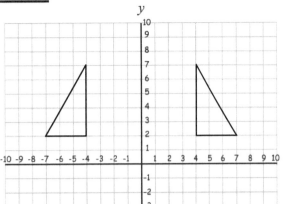

B)

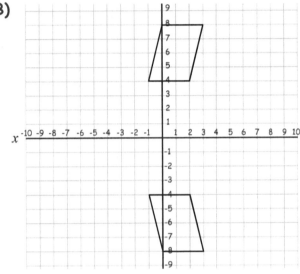

## Page 162:

A)

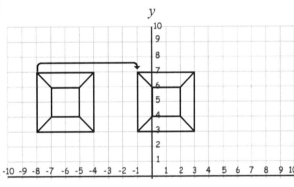

B)

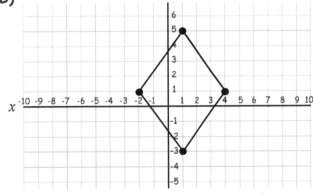

## Page 163:

A)

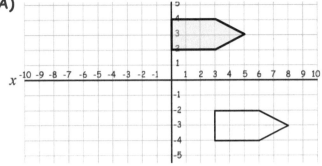

B)

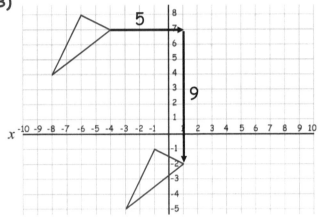

## Page 164:

A)

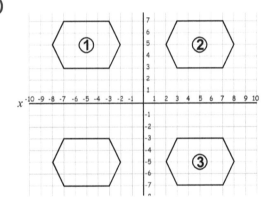

B)

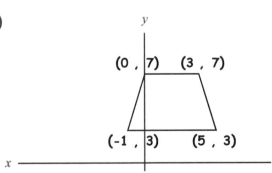

(0 , 7)    (3 , 7)

(-1 , 3)    (5 , 3)

## Page 165:

A)

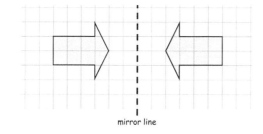

mirror line

B)

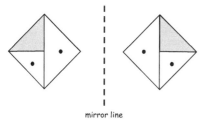

mirror line

## Page 166:

A)

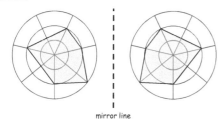

mirror line

B)

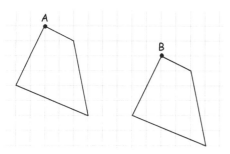

## Page 167:

A)

1. White                    2. Blue

B)

| Team | Angle of section | Number of fans |
|---|---|---|
| England | 120° | **16** |
| France | **60°** | 8 |
| United States | 45° | 6 |
| Ireland | 45° | **6** |
| Spain | **90°** | **12** |

## Page 168:

1. $\dfrac{225}{360} = \dfrac{225 \div 45}{360 \div 45} = \dfrac{5}{8}$   (225° of books)

2. $\dfrac{225}{75} = 3$    140 × 3 = 420 books were sold   (75° of video games)

## Page 169:

1.

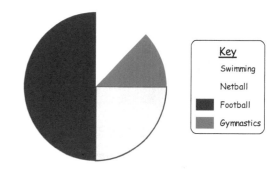

Key
Swimming
Netball
Football
Gymnastics

2. 50%          3. 25% - 12.5% = 12.5%

## Page 170:

1. Just over $\frac{1}{4}$ of 120.

   So, the estimated number of squirrels is 32.

2.    *Johnny*      *Olivia*

3.   Tony found      Olivia found
   $\frac{1}{4}$ of 120 = **30**    $\frac{1}{2}$ of 46 = **23**

## Page 171:

1. April

2. February

3. 85

## Page 172:

1. 10 °C

2. 1 °C

1.

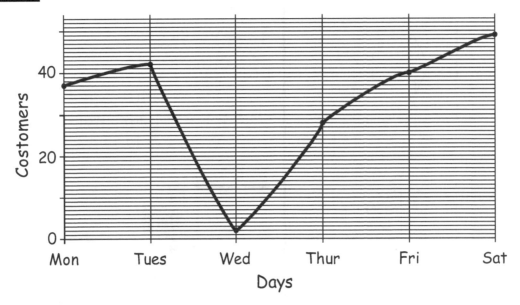

2. Accept an answer between 8.5 and 8.6 Millions.
3. Accept an answer between 9.6 and 9.8 Millions.

**Page 174:**

1.

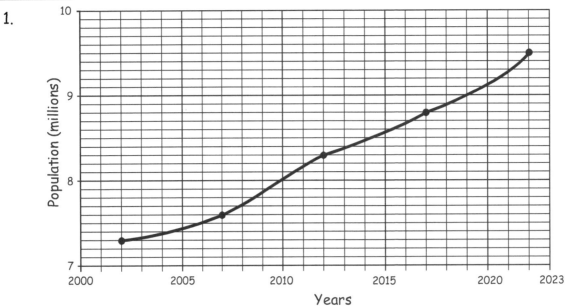

2. Saturday      3. 198 customers.      4. Bad weather (Rain or Snow) – Power cut etc

**Page 175:**

A) 94            B) 35            C) 20 °C

**Page 176:**

A)

1. 3, 5 and 7      2. 1, 2, 5 and 12

3. 1, 2, 3, 7 and 12

B)

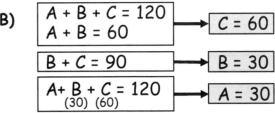

Made in United States
Troutdale, OR
04/27/2024